ANDREW WINTER'S

no-nonsense guide to **buying** and selling property

Wrightbooks

First published 2010 by Wrightbooks
an imprint of John Wiley & Sons Australia, Ltd
42 McDougall Street, Milton Qld 4064

Office also in Melbourne

Typeset in Palatino 11.5/16pt

© Andrew Winter 2010

Reprinted February 2010

The moral rights of the author have been asserted

National Library of Australia Cataloguing-in-Publication data:

Author:	Winter, Andrew.
Title:	No-nonsense guide to buying and selling property / Andrew Winter.
ISBN:	9781742169613 (pbk.)
Notes:	Includes index.
Subjects:	House buying—Australia. House selling—Australia. Home ownership—Australia. Real estate business—Australia.
Dewey Number:	643.12

Cover design by Xou Creative

Cover images by Visual Thing Australia

Andrew Winter is represented by the Harry M Miller Group

As seen on:

The LifeStyle Channel and The LifeStyle Channel logo are registered trademarks of XYZnetworks Pty Limited and used under license.

SELLING HOUSES™ AUSTRALIA is a trademark of Ricochet Limited. This book is not associated with Ricochet Ltd.

Printed in Australia by McPherson's Printing Group

10 9 8 7 6 5 4 3 2

Disclaimer

Contents

About the author

Andrew Winter is obsessed with houses. With 25 years' experience in property he believes that if you haven't sold your house within two months, you're doing something wrong!

Andrew has been selling houses since he was 17 years old, buying his first home at 18, and since then he has experienced all market conditions — good and bad — and sold both beautiful dream homes and houses even the local rat population would steer clear from. His expertise comes from the understanding of the fact that people are actually the main ingredient in the process of buying and selling properties, whether they are first-time owners, seasoned house movers or investors.

Currently based on the Gold Coast, where he lives with his wife and three daughters, British-born Andrew Winter is a real estate agent, property adviser and host of *Selling Houses Australia* — the ASTRA-winning property show on Foxtel and Austar's The LifeStyle Channel.

Acknowledgements

I dedicate this book to my wonderful ex colleague, Mrs Lee Henry. She forwarded my name to the production company back in 2001 (without consulting me first, mind you!) and my success as a television presenter would never have been possible without her. During the writing of this book, Lee sadly lost her battle against a serious illness. She left behind a devoted husband, Dave, a much-loved daughter, Emma, and two grandchildren, who were her absolute pride and joy. Lee, we will all miss you. You will certainly never be forgotten!

There are a few people I'd like to thank:

My Mum and Dad, for keeping the house yellow for years and for refusing to move.

Mike Fudge, my first employer, who gave me a break into the industry.

A big thanks to my gorgeous wife Caroline (aged 29, of course!) and three daughters Olivia, Daisy and Mia. And I couldn't forget our two small annoying dogs and the two guinea pigs named Giggles and Pepper Le Poo (named by the kids). They all put up with me.

Thanks to the Australian Department of Immigration and Citizenship for letting us in.

A huge thanks to The LifeStyle Channel, and the production company and crew for supporting house addicts such as myself across the land.

And of course, I couldn't forget *you*, the lovely reader, for buying and hopefully reading this real estate masterpiece!

Introduction

Why I love houses

For as long as I can remember, I have had a passion for houses. Even as a small child my love for houses knew no bounds— while other toddlers were playing with water pistols, crayons or toy trucks, I was diligently building houses out of Lego blocks.

My childhood interest soon became a fascination with all aspects of the housing industry, including: how we live; what we live in; what makes one person love a style of house and another hate it; why we place so much importance on housing; how a building is made or changed; how a bad home can be made good; and how a building evolves. I love it all.

So, what influenced this attraction? Well, I could claim that it was because I had an impoverished and parentless childhood, was raised by other street urchins in an inner-city slum, and that my dream of living in a normal home rather than a tiny, damp, dark, high-rise government-housing unit was the catalyst that fuelled my life-long interest in houses. However, none of the above is true.

I must confess to being raised in a comfortable, middle-class suburb in a classic English semi. The only possibility that my upbringing could have influenced my infatuation with houses (which in retrospect was rather bizarre, for one so young) is the fact that my parents, being a little older than many parents of the era, were still 'old school' in their attitudes towards housing. That meant we never moved house, and any new furniture purchases or interior changes we made were not only very rare, but also very conservative — and were only ever undertaken through necessity.

In the '70s and early '80s, the exterior of my parents' home was still painted two shades of yellow. The colour scheme was chosen in the '50s or '60s, and had since been dutifully maintained by my father, who saw no need to change something that worked well in his mind. Who can blame him? I, however, found the conservative and outdated tastes of my parents mind-blowingly embarrassing. My antipathy toward the aesthetics of the '50s and '60s made sense, in some ways: the '70s and '80s, which I anticipated with interest and excitement, saw a move toward the heavily materialistic and shallow Western lifestyle that I must admit to absolutely embracing!

My obsession with housing led to a big decision at a young age: I was going to be an architect. I went off to university to enrol. A very nice tutor sat me down and talked me through the list of subjects, the grades I'd require to be accepted and the time involved in doing the course. This was all information I already knew, but now it was *real*. I was 16 — I would not graduate from university until I was 25. I would have had to survive on poorly paid part-time work for the entire period, and once I finally did reach the ancient age of 25, I'd only be at the *bottom* of the architectural tree. My reaction that day was to run. Well, not run *literally*. I got on my bike, cycled the 10 kilometres home and announced to my shattered parents that I was not going to university and the whole architecture deal was off.

Perhaps at this point I should have accepted that I was a slave to materialism, because my other, more conventional, passion was cars. Maybe there is a pattern forming! My father would only ever change a car once he could repair it no more. Whereas my classmates arrived in latest models looking cool, I arrived in an elderly sedan—beautifully maintained, of course—but *so* last decade! I was only a few months away from being able to start driving. The whole study scenario would mean no nice car for me until what seemed like retirement!

Another stroke of bad luck in my teenage eyes was the car sharing that went on with my friend's parents. As I lived 15 kilometres from my senior school, the other car I was delivered to school in was an equally embarrassing vehicle, 15 to 20 years old and more last *century* than last decade. On the days its owners took me to school, I would tell the driver to drop me off around the corner from the school (I claimed I liked the walk).

If ever they were to collect me after school, I had a predetermined location far, far away from the school gates. The driver thought me a nice young lad for undertaking that little extra walk and being conscious of them avoiding the car chaos at the school gate. Little did they know it was no nice thought on my part, just a selfish act to avoid the social stigma of being associated with their vehicle.

Remember, I lived in a yellow house at that time!

Having scrapped the lofty ambition of becoming an architect, I had to consider an alternative career that would allow me to indulge my love of housing *without* spending nine years living a poverty-stricken existence at university. I had always been aware of the world of real estate. At the time that I found myself at the 'career crossroads', estate agents, as they are known in the UK, were mainly family run companies with one office that had been trading for decades, and purely sold houses (rather than their modern counterparts, which sell dreams, lifestyles, finance packages and investments). The men that worked in these companies back then wore tweed, closed at five and did not open on weekends (it was a men-only business back then; now, if more than half a real estate office's staff are not female, something is wrong!).

To me, a life in real estate represented a dream. I'd always wanted to move house—ideally to one *without* yellow windows. It wasn't that I hated our family home—I just wanted to move! Imagine: a job that allowed me to go into numerous properties and to talk about housing all day long. Contrast this excitement about a career in real estate with the ambitions of other 16-year-olds of my generation, who were primarily interested in girls, travel, drinking and living the student lifestyle. Looking back, my unconventional ambition was so strange and so powerful that it might have required psychiatric intervention—but it was my dream, and I was powerless to control it.

My parents were quite rightly unhappy with their only son's decision to ditch a professional career for a life of shallow materialism—funded, at this stage, by pure dreams! Luckily, although my parents were old fashioned in houses, they were pretty damn cool with this situation: no shouting, no screaming and no demands that I must go to university.

Just one simple deal was given to me: I had six months in which to secure a full-time job. At that point, I would have to start paying board and all parental funding would cease. I thought this unfair—I would need at *least* a year to 'find myself' and partake in foreign travel (all on their credit card). But my parents made it perfectly clear that this was not going to happen, so six months it was.

Agents were not exactly jumping over themselves to employ a skinny, 16-year-old youth, so it did take a few tense months before I started landing interviews. (Okay, so *one* interview was all I got.) It was approaching the mid '80s, and there was a change in the air which, I suspect, lead to my first lucky break. One agent eventually took the plunge when he saw me. This man was an instant idol for me: he could go into people's homes anywhere in the city. How fab was that?

My new mentor was from an emerging breed of '80s real estate agents who, unlike their earlier counterparts, did not operate in a family run company with one humble office that closed at five every day. This guy had 20 offices as part of his company, which was unheard of back then, and this was no franchise—he *personally* owned 20 branches across the city. He said he would give me a chance as a trainee—the youngest they had ever had. Within a matter of months, in January 1984, I started work in the world of real estate.

I worked very long hours, but I loved it so much that time was not an issue. My God, I was in heaven! Houses by day, and a cool company car to pose in by night (admittedly, I was hardly ever not at work for those first few years).

I didn't earn much that first year as I continually managed to drive my shiny company car into random bollards, gate posts and even another parked car, so much of my earnings were handed back to the company's insurers.

And so my career in real estate began. I managed to move around the country trying new locations, and by the mid '90s I started working in central London. I had worked hard in the industry for years making a reasonable living, which was boosted by my rapid climb up the property ladder. As I really did enjoy the work, I had unwittingly become very knowledgeable about the subject of real estate. Now, some people might accuse me of being cocky, so I should point out that not many people who have done one job for a long time, and who love that job and who have undertaken the role in many different marketplaces, could really be anything other than knowledgeable.

In 2001, an opportunity would present itself to me that would change my career—and my life—forever. A TV production company was looking for a property expert who was obsessed by houses. A lovely colleague of mine put my name forward for the gig without telling me. Thinking I would be asked to appear on one episode of a show I had not yet heard about, I went along to the interview—which, incidentally, I thought went terribly. Not so. I was informed later that day that I'd been chosen, not to be *interviewed* for a property show as I had thought, but to *host* a property show!

Originally, I had little interest in the role—I didn't even really know what was involved. In fact, the first year was pure hell, because I was completely outside my comfort zone. I only knew about houses, and although the show was about my favourite subject, people watching me doing my work was something I had not experienced since I was 17 or 18!

Selling Houses was born in early 2002, and over the following years, it became a huge success, being viewed by millions of people in the UK on prime time TV. To my complete shock and horror, people started recognising me in public. Still, it was worth it. I got to see more houses and meet more people than ever before, and I had the opportunity to travel throughout Europe and, since 2007, Australia.

It was late in 2006 that an employee of The LifeStyle Channel holidaying on the Gold Coast noticed that the host of their overseas property show seemed to be living down under. This information was passed to one of the channel's programmers, and the result was *Selling Houses Australia*. How lucky was that?

Selling Houses has been a wonderful opportunity for me—not because it gets me on the TV (I never wanted that), but because it has allowed me to see into a huge variety of homes in many different locations. It has also given me the opportunity to be honest with people without fear of losing my job or risking a seller listing their home with another agent—the number one fear for any good agent! It may be a TV show, but we really do sell the houses, so it is like a dream situation for a passionate agent.

I frequently meet agents with five or 10 years' experience in real estate. Rarely do I meet agents with more than 20 years' experience and, when I do, it is even rarer for the person to have experience working in many different housing markets. The fact that I became one of these rare creatures of extensive and broad experience was not planned—it evolved. I would get to know a housing market inside out, then feel the need to move on. I did urban, I did cheap, I did expensive, I did country. I even did good old suburban.

In recent years, it has been the fascinating Aussie housing market that has received my full attention. I have lived in Australia with my wife and three girls since 2005, on the northern fringes of the Gold Coast. In our first three years here, we owned and operated a real estate business (what else could I do?) and since 2008 I have concentrated on media work and property consultancy.

In the volatile and unpredictable world of Australian real estate, it's often hard to make the right decisions when buying or selling your property. My experience in the Australian housing market has given me a great deal of insight into the common practices of professionals working in the housing industry, from real estate agents to developers. Unfortunately, there are agents who can't be trusted and can be plain useless. Equally, there are many very good and trustworthy agents who will always do their best—it's so rewarding to meet a client who is obviously on guard about the type of agent you are, who ends up being delighted because of the fantastic job you've done. Of course, no matter how much effort you put in there will always be clients who still blame you when everything goes wrong! But that is one of the pitfalls of the role. Funnily enough, people never complain they were misled when the value of their home increases! To further complicate the process of buying or selling a house, the market changes constantly. During my career, I have witnessed the continual movement of the housing market: the '70s, '80s, '90s and the 'noughties' have all had highs and lows.

So much has evolved in the industry in the last five years, but the biggest change is in the public's interest in the subject. Financing, plus the technology and information available, has led to a whole new world.

These complexities are the basis for my motivation for writing this book. I have compiled a basic introduction to the world of real estate, as seen through my experienced and very sceptical eyes.

I want this book to portray the truth about real estate. I have always had a direct approach and a very fair and honest out-look, and I can happily claim to have sold literally thousands and thousands of homes, and not *once* have I sold a home where either the seller or the buyer has unknowingly lost out or been conned.

My honest and direct approach will help you confidently negotiate your way through the many obstacles you'll face when dealing with the Australian property market.

I wish you all the best in buying your new home or selling your existing one!

Andrew Winter
On the set of *Selling Houses Australia*
December 2009

On your marks, get set...

Chapter 1

Are you ready to buy a home?

By the time I was 18, I felt 100 per cent ready to buy my first home—in fact, I could barely think of anything else. As far as I could see, the pros of buying were that I had a long-standing career (nearly 10 whole months) in real estate behind me, I had a tiny deposit saved and I had a desperate desire to own bricks and mortar. A few negatives were also floating around in my head at the time, as I recall. These included parental shock and horror, a decided lack of annual income and my youth and inexperience—I certainly did not know of anyone else that had bought their first home at the age of 18!

I soon forgot about the negatives when I found my first dream home by accident. I was working in a modern suburban area that was popular with first-time homebuyers, and I spent most evenings driving excited clients around a selection of homes. These first-homeowners-to-be would eventually settle on either the smartest house they saw, or the cheapest—that seemed to be the deal back then. During this period, I kept showing clients one particular home. It was neither the smartest nor the cheapest, so no-one wanted it.

After showing the home to yet another uninterested client, I asked my boss for more information about the house at number six. Why, in his wisdom, did he think everyone was refusing its charms?

'It's obvious', he retorted. 'Number six is a hellhole.'

Well, he was right. Ten years before, the owner had bought number six as a brand-new house with his loving wife—who unfortunately happened to be loving someone else at the same time. Said wife left the owner in the house during their first year together, leaving him alone with his motorbike and his large and rather odorous dog.

The house featured three bedrooms—well, one bedroom (read: camping ground) and two rooms full of junk—one bathroom that looked like it had last been cleaned when his loving wife left him nine years previously, a lounge room that was carpeted in a colour that was now undistinguishable because of the motorbike and its parts that were housed there. It had a kitchen decorated in a tasteful style reminiscent of a '70s roadhouse. Outside, the paint was faded, and the yard—well, that was just another place for bike parts. The garage was tidy for some strange reason. The interior smelled of dog, cigarette smoke, dirt and grease—baking fresh bread to impress prospective buyers would have been a waste of time here!

I had seen loads of homes in this suburb by this point. Although I was in England at the time and the homes were obviously sold in pounds sterling, I will convert the prices to Aussie dollars for the sake of clarity. The cheap grotty homes in poor blocks in poorer streets fetched the equivalent of between $34 000 and $36 000 and good homes in better streets got between $44 000 and $46 000. Number six was in one of the better streets but, as my boss had put it so beautifully, was a hellhole. Blind to his home's shabby condition, the owner had priced it at $41 000.

A few more frantic sales weeks passed by and I began to take more notice of this ugly duckling, as I showed more dreamed-up homebuyers through number six and they continued to refuse its attractions. Some did not even venture to the upper level. Meanwhile, the bank was knocking on the owner's door and telling him to pay up or get out.

One fateful evening my boss took a call from the owner of number six—which I overheard. The owner really needed to sell, and had decided he might consider a lower offer.

Taking a deep breath, I boldly spoke up. 'Could I buy number six? I will offer him $36 000.' The office went quiet, bar a few rude remarks regarding my age.

'I want to buy it', I repeated.

'Have you got $36 000?' my boss asked.

'No,' I said, 'but can't I get one of those mortgages like everyone else?'

The next two months were not easy. My parents had only just got over the shock of their teenage son ditching his career in architecture, and now he was about to take out a big mortgage! To make things even worse, getting the mortgage was not easy. Our in-house financial department spent a lot of time convincing the lender to let me have the loan, and I believe some adjustments to my projected salary may have been made.

Despite all that, I knew I was ready to buy that house. I got it for $37 000 and tidied it up with a lot of help from my wonderful father; I think at this point Dad had accepted my real estate addiction and became a massive help in the early years of housing renovations. The news got better, too! Number six sold 10 months later for $51 500.

Although I didn't plan for this process, it is generally a good idea to have a careful plan in place before you undertake a project such as this one. This chapter outlines all the planning you'll need to do to buy your first home, as I did with number six.

What is the commitment?

So are you ready to buy a house? You are probably ready if you:

- believe you have a relatively steady income source for the future, and are prepared to change careers if you need to

- have a 'get out quick' plan for when things go wrong

- feel as though it is the right time for you

- are prepared to sacrifice all your free time in exchange for either working on the house or staying in because you can't afford to go out.

In other words, you must be prepared to make a commitment.

Are you ready emotionally?

If an agent asks you how long you have been househunting for, or how many homes you have inspected, he or she is trying to establish whether you are emotionally ready to buy. If your search has taken more than six months, or you have inspected 50 or more homes, *you are not ready*! Trust me: if you have done your research and really targeted your search, there won't even *be* 50 homes to inspect. So ditch the deal until you really are ready.

Obviously, the financial commitment of buying a home is key, but this comes with a range of emotional issues that you must take into account. All your spare money will be taken up in the first few years, not only with mortgage repayments but also with running costs, improvements and furnishings. This means less money for going out and partying. So does that mean boredom? I didn't think so, and the kudos it gave me among my peers was worth it. But owning a home is a never-ending cycle of financial commitment, and you cannot escape that.

Who can hinder you?

As an agent, the first-time purchaser's parents are always the people we dread most on inspections. These interventionist, nosy folk have delivered the kiss of death to many a deal. I have to tell you (but don't tell them!) that, in most cases, their advice is ill informed and sometimes just completely wrong. So watch out, and don't let your folks influence your emotions too much!

Maybe I am being a bit harsh on the mums and dads out there. As a parent myself, I will of course be offering my offspring advice — but my advice will be right, of course. The agents will take one look at me and give in!

Comments to watch out for include:

- 'You don't want to buy *there*, do you dear?'
- 'I remember houses here that used to be $100 000 and you couldn't *give* them away!'
- 'Do you *really* like this place? Hmmm, okay…'

It is not just parents who can give you misleading advice and influence your emotions regarding the house of your dreams — it can be your friends, too. Some people enjoy nothing more than going along with you and throwing in a good 'tut tut' and a cutting sarcastic comment here and there.

The key when dealing with meddlers is to trust your own opinions and thoughts. If you have researched all the elements, you will be fine.

Are you ready financially?

The ability of first homebuyers to afford their first home is always being reported on in the media — each generation claiming that it is harder for them to get on the property ladder than it was for the last generation. These observations are accurate in part but, in my experience, financial limitations can be solved by buying what you can afford and not being bloody-minded about the process. First homebuyers need to acknowledge the limitations of their budget: demanding certain features in their first home or insisting on certain suburbs — all because you think you *must* have these things — won't get you anywhere, so get real with your expectations.

When you think you are ready emotionally for the commitment, start the process of working out how much you can afford. You should ask yourself the following questions:

- 🏠 Do I have a deposit?

- 🏠 How much can I afford to pay to the bank each month? (Remember that you may be able to afford a certain amount now, but it's always best to borrow less than your maximum limit, just in case your income or incomes reduce for some reason or interest rates increase.)

- 🏠 Do I have an adequate fallback plan?

- 🏠 Do I have other financial commitments such as car loans or credit cards, and if so, am I sure I can manage a mortgage on top of these debts?

If you're unsure whether you can afford a mortgage, try a month-long 'dummy run'. This is where you practise living as if you have had the expense of a mortgage each month on top of your regular expenditure. Can you live on the remainder — really?

As tedious as this all sounds, you really need to do your homework. Do not over commit, and ensure you're not paying too much for something you could have found cheaper elsewhere.

Who can help you?

There are many people whose services can be of great help to an aspiring homeowner when attempting to untangle the complicated world of buying property. As with everything else in life, everyone has a particular angle or agenda that may influence the type of advice they give you, so always consider this element when accepting advice from professionals. Following are some of the people whose advice might be relevant when making decisions about buying a home, and a discussion of what agenda they may be pushing.

Lenders

Many home loans in Australia will be dealt with by the major banks. These organisations will have a variety of mortgage products, but they will always be limited to offering their products only. Be sure to shop around for the best deal.

Mortgage brokers

A mortgage broker or agent will help you to research the best mortgage package for you. Because they are not affiliated with one institution, they might have a broader perspective on what's out there, and be able to give you a less biased opinion than a bank might.

Financial planners

Financial planners review your overall financial position and take this into account when helping you decide what kind of mortgage will best suit your needs. Check that these guys are not pushing a certain product. Make sure you back up their opinion with your own research.

Accountants

Accountants are able to advise you on the tax implications of your decisions, and help you budget. They can also be a great source of impartial advice, and can help you review the options you have been given by other advisers. Accountants are less likely than other experts to have a hidden agenda, so they're less likely to steer you towards a particular package because they have something to gain from it. You pay for their time, so when you meet with them, be prepared with your questions and paperwork.

Lawyers

It is always worthwhile using a lawyer when purchasing a home. They can interpret contracts, advise you on the local regulations that govern your purchase and steer you away from potentially dodgy vendors.

> **Conveyancers versus lawyers**
>
> Lawyers are the most expensive option, but have a vast array of expertise on hand. They are arguably in the best position when things start to get tricky. For uncomplicated deals, use a conveyancer. They are licensed and specialise in property transactions only, so can be a great alternative. Often they are a bit cheaper than a lawyer, too.

Buyer's agents

Buyer's agents work on behalf of the buyer to research and inspect properties, then negotiate prices with the seller. These agents act for buyers only, and get paid directly by the buyer once a home has been secured. There is generally no conflict of interest here, although buyers' agents can get commissions from agents. These commissions must be declared at the start of the process.

Have you set a budget?

Your budget should always be set in consultation with an accountant or broker, who will be familiar with the current economic and legal landscape in which you are buying. Your lender or broker will ask you to consider the following things when setting a budget:

- price of house
- deposit amount
- acquisition costs
- stamp duty
- legal costs
- advance strata fees
- monthly running costs

- 🏠 mortgage
- 🏠 insurances
- 🏠 rates
- 🏠 strata levies.

The reason your budget must be the first issue tackled before buying is that it will dictate all your subsequent decisions: the suburb you can buy in, the size of home or unit you can choose and the features you can afford.

Ensure that once you've taken all these costs into account, you are still able to live comfortably on your available income.

Borrow less than you are offered

Remember, when setting your budget, it's important to allow yourself some leeway to account for possible unforseen setbacks, such as career changes, job loss, relationship breakdowns, unexpected emergency spending or rising interest rates. Let's say, for example, that the bank allows you and your partner to borrow $300000. In this situation, I would be borrowing between $250000 and $275000, to ensure you have a considerable comfort zone.

Consider your attitude to risk, and think about what you would do if your income dropped or ceased. Sometimes it is worth borrowing less than the lenders will actually lend to give you some peace of mind. If you are a natural risk taker, or the home at the top end of your budget appears to be worth the risk, prepare a backup plan.

Financing your new purchase

Having ascertained that you have a reasonable deposit, a stable job, a backup plan in case of emergency and a realistic idea of what you can expect to pay (based on consultation with experts), it's time to investigate how to pay for your new house.

Researching your options

As tedious as it sounds, the key to being in the best financial position to buy a house is research. It's important to do your homework, which means utilising the help of advisers such as the ones mentioned on pages 7 and 8 to work out how much you can afford to spend, and which mortgage structure suits you best. My golden rule here is to ask lots of questions. The reason you need to talk to lots of different advisers and ask them questions *before* you find your home is so you can do your research without pressure. You are a first-time buyer, and you do have time—so check out all your options and you'll reduce the chances of things going wrong.

You can also do some online research to familiarise yourself with the legal and economic landscape in which you're buying.

Choosing the right mortgage

The term 'mortgage structure' sounds complicated, so think of it in its purest sense: it is a long-term loan that is, almost without exception, the cheapest form of borrowing available. Different lenders will offer you a multitude of packages or products, each sporting a new and appealing feature.

Your first decision will be on the length of the loan. The longer the loan's term, the lower your monthly interest repayments will be—but the more interest you'll pay overall. So a 20-year loan will cost you more each month, but less overall, than a 30-year loan.

The next thing to consider will be the repayment structure. There are a multitude of things to consider here, so don't be afraid to ask questions of your lender or any of the other experts you've enlisted to assist you.

Fixed-rate loans

Fixed-rate deals, where a home loan is repaid at the same (fixed) interest rate for a period of time, can be great; they are easy to budget for in the first year or two, and you know your payments will not change from month to month. But fixed-rate deals usually involve paying penalties if you need to get out of the arrangement or sell your home—so make sure you know what these terms are, and how long any penalties continue.

There is another negative: when paying back a fixed-rate loan, you always pay the same interest rate, no matter what the economy's doing. This is great if general rates continue to rise, because you're still paying the same fixed rate that you agreed to when you took out the mortgage. But often, fixed-rate loans mean you'll pay a slightly higher level of interest than people on a variable-rate loan.

Check where the interest rates are in their cycle: if rates look set to increase, it may be a good time to get a fixed-interest loan. To find out more about interest rates and their current levels, check online at <www.rba.gov.au>.

Variable-rate loans

Variable-rate loans, which carry an interest rate that may move up or down depending on the movements of the economy, will usually give you total flexibility and a lower monthly rate at the time you take out the mortgage. Beware, though, that the rates can change every time the bank decides to adjust its rates. Remember, when you hear the news that your bank has increased its rate by 1 per cent, your $300 000 variable-rate mortgage that was costing you $1500 per month will now be $1750 per month. So you must be sure you can cope with unexpected increases. Of course, the reverse is true: if rates drop, you benefit.

Interest-only versus principal-and-interest loans

When working out the repayment structure, there are so many things to consider! Do you pay the interest only, or should you always pay off the loan combined with the interest?

The latter is the more costly option. On a $300000 interest-only loan, the payments would be $1500 at 6 per cent. On a principal-and-interest scheme, you'd pay $1932.

In simple terms, an interest-only loan is a loan where you repay only the interest on the principal during the loan's term. At the end of that time — usually one to five years — you repay the amount you borrowed as a lump sum. As you would expect, repayments are lower than with a standard principal-and-interest loan. In practice this means that if you borrow $300000, at the end of the term (say, five years), you will still owe the lender $300000.

If you combine interest while paying off the loan itself, at the end of the term (usually much longer — 20- to 30-year mortgages are not uncommon) you owe nothing. The repayments on this type of mortgage are much more.

The reason so many people opt for interest-only loans is to keep monthly costs down. Another incentive is the hope that the home's value will increase substantially by the time you need to pay the loan back. The decision is usually about whether or not you can afford to pay off the principal. If you can, a principle-and-interest loan is the best choice.

Redundancy protection

Redundancy protection is a form of insurance that you can link to your loan to cover any shortfalls in income if you are ever made redundant. These policies vary substantially, so research thoroughly and compare each deal.

Mortgage holidays

A mortgage holiday is not where your lender sends you to Bali once a year — all expenses paid. A mortgage holiday is a gap in monthly payments for a set time. It can be an effective way of planning for life's little unexpected disasters, but be aware that to finance this gap in monthly payments, the lender will usually have to increase the cost of your repayments.

Shopping around for the best deal

Having decided on the best mortgage structure for your needs, shop around for the best mortgage packages available. You might approach a lender directly and use a broker or two. Compare what they have to offer you, and don't be afraid to tell them what other lenders are offering you for equivalent products—you might be able to talk the lender into giving you a better deal.

. . . .

What's the agent thinking?

If you turn up to inspections with your best friend—or, even worse, your parents—watch the agent's reactions: they will either be totally resigned to the fact that no deal will be done today, or they will embark on a wonderful array of sales techniques aimed purely at your parents. Do not be shocked if they ignore you entirely. The younger you are (or the younger you look), the more gullible the agent will think you are. Have fun with the agent— let him or her think you are gullible. Don't tell them you have read this book! If this happens, try to remember that as a first-time purchaser with finances in place and emotions intact, you are actually a very desirable commodity and good agents will know this.

Another little trick us agents like to play is 'becoming your mate'. Good service is key and you should expect it, but note that agents are paid by the seller. Some agents will think by 'becoming your mate' you will suddenly throw caution to the wind and sign up for anything they tell you to.

Pick me!
Pick me!

Chapter 2

*Finding and buying
your perfect home*

As you know, I discovered my first home when I was working as a real estate agent, while showing prospective buyers around it. My background research had been unwittingly completed in the months of hard work and late-night inspections with prospective buyers that had preceded my purchase: I had viewed most of the competition.

So my real house-hunting expertise was not consolidated until I bought my second house. I had already put house number one on the market. Why? I really can't remember! Maybe it was because I had owned it for nearly 10 months, had renovated extensively and had already grown bored of it. I was young! Nevertheless, I decided to sell. My first house was sold the very day I put it on the market—but that, too, is another story.

So there I was, now at the dizzy and mature age of 19, about to hand over the keys to my first home and I needed to buy a new house quick smart—but where to begin?

I started with the question of price: I did the usual financial checks and shopped around to find some suitable finance packages, so I knew what my budget was.

The next item to consider was *where* to buy. I wanted to stay in the same suburb in which I'd lived in my first home; I wanted to be close to my friends and family. It was a marketplace I knew well.

Then, for the first time in my life, I had the great pleasure of officially starting to look for a house. That meant visiting displays and established homes, picking the brains of real estate agents and embarking on all the other trappings of searching for a home. Now I know that the very idea of searching for a new house can fill some people with horror—so I was lucky that I relished the thought. In fact, this time around I found the process of house hunting very empowering, because I knew that I really could make a decision if I wanted to. In fact, I was quite annoyed when within merely a week I had already tracked down my new home.

Although I had been conducting house inspections with prospective buyers for nearly two years, I had never experienced the other side of the fence. I had great fun. In that era—the mid '80s—some real estate agents would let you go around to their clients' homes on your own. As I often worked late, the evening inspections were all I could fit into my schedule. When I'd go to inspect a property in the evening, it wasn't other agents conducting the inspections—it was the proud homeowners themselves who undertook this task, and wow! What an array of tactics, procedures and methodologies they displayed.

Usually, if a couple owned the house, the woman of the house would reluctantly take on the task of showing me around the home and all its delights. Unfortunately, due to my budget, we were not talking 'spacious homes' with rooms and rooms—so the tours the women took me on could be very quick and, before the man of the house had a chance to hide his ashtray and spray some air freshener around the living room, we would be back to the room we started in. The nervous partner would always ask me: 'What do you think, mate? We love it!' I would stop myself from replying with: 'If you like it, then why are you selling it? And no, I think this is probably the last place in this suburb I would consider buying'. I did not say this—rather, I would say that I loved it and would give it some more thought and go back to the agent, usually followed by a comment about popping back to see the house again in the following days (the sellers' faces always lit up on this note). I never meant it, of course—but how can you tell people their home has less style than a bogan's rumpus room?

These homeowners were fascinating. In observing their techniques, I noticed that they seemed to focus exclusively on one approach: the great undersell (where the seller plays up the negative features of the home to avoid nasty surprises for the buyer). I surmised that they planned not to bother with 'the big sell', relying instead on the number of people they managed to attract. I imagine they hoped that if they got enough people through the door, at some point someone would say 'yes' to their unexciting, gloomy abode.

Of course, my search for a home also included inspections with professional real estate agents. These experiences, too, gave me valuable insights into the industry in which I worked. Despite having spent two years working in real estate, I was unprepared for the shock of meeting the agents as a buyer. As you know, agents vary substantially, ranging from the meek and mild who speak only when pushed, to the big, brash and flash, who are so pushy you could smack them one. Some of them care, some do not—some make you wonder how they would ever be able to sell anybody anything.

Eventually—well, a whole week later—an agent was successful in convincing me to buy. My purchase was a brand-new home from a display complex. When I think back on it now, I recall that the sales person was smart, efficient and polite, and had a discreet but strong sales technique. He listened and asked questions, and made me feel good about the whole process, and the house itself. Needless to say, I fell for these clever tactics—pay attention all you agents out there, you might learn something!

To all prospective homebuyers, I offer the following advice: before you start looking for a *property*, remember that you are looking for your *home*. This means you need to take into account what you want from the land, the structure upon it, the home's environment and the suburb in which it's located. In terms of the community you'll be moving into, remember that the only people who count in the long run are your closest neighbours, and you usually won't get to meet them until the deal is done and dusted.

How do you start looking for your first home?

Now that my rant is over, I can suggest to you the most logical order in which to approach the task of hunting for your new home. You should approach the matter in the following order:

- 🏠 Work out your price range.
- 🏠 Choose a location.
- 🏠 Make a 'wishlist' of specifications.

Working out your price range

Now is the time to put your research to good use and decide on a realistic price range. The price you decide on will dictate every element of your planned search, so it must be decided before you do anything else. Remember, as I outlined in chapter 1, before deciding on a price you should consult your finance broker, contact your lender directly and do extensive research online. Never be pushed into over-committing yourself. This is the time to set your price bracket and be prepared to stick to it.

Are you in a buyers' or a sellers' market?

Pay close attention to the market conditions at the time of your search. Are you in a buyers' or a sellers' market?

A buyers' market is defined by an abundance of housing stock, but not a huge amount of demand for the stock. This means there will be plenty of choice for the buyer. Some indicators of a buyers' market are low property prices and sellers that are keen to negotiate a lower figure for their home. There may also be low auction clearance rates, and an abundance of 'for sale' boards and property ads stating discounts.

A sellers' market is the exact opposite. This is where there is very little housing stock for sale, but a large demand for that small amount of housing stock. You can tell if you're in a sellers' market because sellers won't be willing to negotiate on price, there will be high auction clearance rates and 'sold' boards will be everywhere.

For example, if you are in a sellers' market and your budget is $300 000, forget looking at houses listed at $325 000—the seller is not likely to reduce his or her price. However, if your house hunt is taking place in a buyers' market, you should consider inspecting homes listed as high as $350 000. This is because if you are in an economic climate favourable to buyers, the seller is more likely to reduce the asking price—especially if he or she has been trying to sell for a long time.

At the other end of the scale, look from $200 000 upwards just in case a renovation project or bargain pops up. This is more likely to happen in a buyers' market purely because sellers become desperate after lengthy periods on the market, so some homes can be massively reduced.

Choosing a location

The sooner you can narrow down your search criteria, the more effective your search will be. It is important to realise that the property market is a big place, and virtually every suburb has its own 'micro market'—pockets of high and low growth, or areas within the suburb that are better suited to your needs for some reason or another. In my experience, people often select location prior to establishing their price range, which makes no sense, because quite often your budget may rule out your selected suburb and your search will start and end with disappointment.

Your budget may have narrowed down your options, but you'll need to move forward by selecting areas within your chosen suburb that you know and like, or areas that you know are good localities because you have friends or family living there.

Most people are now familiar with the term 'hot spot'. It is a term created for investors, and relates to the profitability of buying in a particular suburb for the purpose of later selling at a profit. Don't allow yourself to focus on future growth or investment potential too much when selecting your location. Your priority should be that you buy a place that you will enjoy living in — and not because its median house values increased 6 per cent in the last quarter and the media claims that this is a top area. If you select an area because it is right for you (short of buying a house with a sewage works next door, or in a suburb where all the other homes in the area are being bulldozed for a nuclear power plant), the growth in value of your suburb should keep up with everyone else's, provided that you've chosen well within that area.

For this reason, you need to get to know your selected search area intimately. I guarantee you that suburbs you hear about featuring 'amazing growth' will still contain some homes that performed poorly. Furthermore, if the suburb's growth is already being reported on, you are too late to get the 'deal of a lifetime' the media is promising you, and you could even be buying at the top of the market. So relax. Select an area carefully but select it because you like it, or it works for you as a base. The local council may be able to help you choose by confirming that no new plans that could be detrimental to the suburb are in the planning process. Ask around — don't be scared to talk to the neighbours. They will always moan or sing an area's praises without prejudice.

Making a wishlist of specifications

When agents talk about 'specifications', we're talking about the type of house you want: its condition (renovated or unrenovated), design, materials, number of bedrooms or bathrooms, size, character, garden and so on. The specifications of the house should be considered after both the price range and the location have been established, because both will dictate the style and size of home you can go for. For example, your decision to avoid borrowing all the money offered by the lender, or to buy within five kilometres of the CBD, may mean that you can now only afford a one-bedroom unit (rather than a three-bedroom house). Perhaps you originally wanted a character-filled period home, but the suburbs in your financial reach are featuring more recently built homes. To make your search work, and to avoiding taking six months or a year to find a home, you need to be realistic and flexible. If you cannot afford a three-bedroom freestanding home in your preferred suburb, buy a two-bedroom unit instead—just make sure you've searched thoroughly and found the best one out there. Alternatively, if you need three bedrooms, move suburbs to allow for more square metres for your dollar. But don't spend months and months moaning about the market. Just get on with your search and adapt to suit your criteria.

Remember that housing is the only product in our modern world where the buying process is not as simple as deciding what you want, checking that you can afford it and then buying it. Buying a house will always be about compromise. Even if you decide to build your own house from scratch, the land you choose will be dictated by availability and your budget. Similarly, the house's design will be dictated by the land you've been able to acquire and, of course, your budget.

Carefully consider the limitations of your wishlist

You'll need to consider your limitations when deciding on the specifications of your new home. For example, are you willing to live in an unrenovated house? If so, would you know how to undertake works to upgrade it yourself, or do you have family and friends who could help you? Assuming you can do the renovations on your own, are you willing to give up enough time to undertake the improvements? Be honest with yourself. A three-bedroom home may be your dream, but being unable to afford a renovated three-bedroom and opting for an *unrenovated* three-bedroom that you hope to update may not be the right option—the house may need extensive and costly renovations, and making the changes yourself might take all your spare time and money. Buying a renovated two-bedroom unit instead might get you on the property ladder, allow you to retain free time and be easier to budget for. You need to know what will work best for you.

Remember, larger houses involve hidden costs that don't apply to smaller ones, for several reasons:

- they cost more to furnish

- they take more time to maintain

- they have higher council rates.

I know it looks better to be the proud owner of a big house, but it's no fun if you can't afford to live in it comfortably.

 Sample wishlist

Here is an example of my wishlist for an investment property that I purchased last year:

▲ *Location*. I chose a suburb that I liked and knew well, because I had a fair idea of how the market worked and felt comfortable there.

▲ *Price*. My choice of suburb dictated my price, as did my budget. I wanted to enter the lower end of my chosen suburb's market to ensure that capital growth would be strong.

▲ *Rooms*. I wanted four bedrooms and two bathrooms to ensure ease of rental and future resale.

▲ *Specifications*. I wanted a home that had special features that gave it character and made it aesthetically appealing.

▲ Most importantly, I wanted a seller very keen to sell.

This sounds like a tall order, but this search took less than a week. Because I knew what I wanted, I recognised it as soon as I found it. After a few drive-bys and one inspection, the deal was done.

A fascinating fact that I've grown to understand over the years is that these perceptions towards negatives vary vastly from place to place. Buyers in some areas see a feature that affects their housing stock as acceptable, whereas buyers in other areas find the very same element a problem. For example, main roads rarely have a negative impact on inner-city unit buildings, but the same feature will have a negative impact on prices in a normally quiet suburb with tree-lined streets. Power lines are unpopular, but if half the residents of the suburb have sight of them, the negative becomes 'normal', and buyers become used to this 'feature'—so its impact is greatly reduced.

If a property features a particularly negative element (such as a power line or multi-lane highway out the front, or industrial buildings nearby), ensure the price you pay is considerably less than a similar home would be if it was 500 metres away in a much nicer street.

They say size does matter, but even that isn't strictly true in the world of property. What passes for 'normal sized' in one suburb might be considered unacceptably small in another. The rule here is if something that you would consider detrimental is seen in the majority of homes in your search area, you probably don't need to worry too much about its effect on future property values.

When weighing up the negatives of the home, remember that you have to live there and put up with any negative elements—so only compromise as much as you can tolerate.

Last year I helped some very good friends of ours select a new home. Their wishlist and their budget matched, but this was to be a long-term family home and they wanted to ensure not only that the wishlist was adhered to, but also that the home felt right. That 'right feeling' is impossible to define as it is different for everyone, but you will know when you feel it—it's like love really, you just know it is right. (Okay, so it can end in a divorce, but at least if you start right you've got a chance!)

These friends knew the suburbs they wanted, and they knew exactly what kind of house they wanted: a freestanding four-bedroom home with two bathrooms, two living areas on a nice street. You would be amazed at how many homes met these criteria on the internet and in agents' windows, but on inspection just did not feel right. On our search, we discovered that another wishlist feature was decent ceiling height and some architectural character or interest. After a few heavy inspection sessions, they got very excited about a home that seemed to meet all their criteria. Its only issue was that its outdoor covered area was tiny and hard to extend. They submitted an offer, but the seller was not exactly coming to the party on price or terms. As negotiations continued, I could see our mates slowly falling out of love with the home.

At this point I recalled a home we had all inspected, that they had really fallen in love with—but because the house only had one living area, it had been discarded. So I persuaded my friends to take another look at that house with one living area. We all went over one Saturday morning, and the moment they stepped back into this home, they made all the right buyer noises: lots of oooohhhs, sighs and smiles—the kids ran around with happy faces. We had a brief discussion about how you could create a second living area. As it turned out creating a second living area was not only possible, but it would add future value.

It was decided this was a compromise they were prepared to make because everything else was ticked: the high ceilings, the fantastic outdoor area, the home's location, its architectural style—it was just what this family wanted. This was a big compromise, but the difference here is the compromise could be rectified at some point. The cost of the changes would be easily covered by an increased sale value. This contrasts starkly with the previous example, where the compromises were too complicated and expensive to overcome at a later date. The second family bought wisely because they bought a home they loved, and continue to love. They have no regrets about the first home they offered on. This wise buy is the safer investment, too. Why? Because the lack of a second living space can be dealt with.

Making compromises

Recently I went to see a home that a family had purchased a year or so before, following an interstate move. The family loved boats, but a waterfront block was not in their budget, so they made the sensible choice and went for a home near rather than on the water — in a waterfront estate with a marina facility on hand. They even managed to secure one of the only houses that had a water view (across the road, but a view nonetheless). On the surface, this seemed like a very understandable decision and a great example of compromise.

I can imagine how the inspection went: they saw the block position and fell in love, did a quick tally of the number of rooms and decided to purchase. Sure, the kitchens and bathrooms were not their style, and the home itself failed to deliver on the 'wow' factor, but the fact it was a bland home in a great spot passed them by. Careful thought would have revealed that although the block and size were right, the home itself lacked the fittings they wanted, and the floor plan created dark rooms. Only two rooms in the house — the study and the formal lounge — benefited from the wonderful view. To alter the floor plan and fittings would be very costly and difficult. Their desire for a view had blighted their selection, and now although they love the view, they really hate the home. They are already planning very costly renovations and another move in a few years.

The reason this compromise did not work is simple: the compromise was too big. The home didn't meet the family's needs and the interior just did not excite them. The same home without the water view would have been much cheaper. The worst part is that with the cost of moving and renovating, they could nearly have afforded the waterfront home they wanted.

Househunting 101

If you have read this far and are still keen to buy, it's time to start looking for your perfect property. Before jumping in, it's very important to think carefully about what your goals are and research the market in your chosen locale meticulously.

Researching the market

Thorough research is the single most important thing you can do to maximise your chances of meeting your goals when buying a new home. Your research can be done by searching property sites online, through face-to-face meetings with agents and by looking at the property sections of newspapers or the free magazines that are available at real estate offices.

Bear in mind the importance of keeping up to date with your research. All 'previous sales' research you do is of course historical —okay, it may only be a few months old—but that can be a long time in the property market. Don't get confused or mislead by the information. Whereas professional valuers and agents know how to interpret the results in their proper context, the general 'public' doesn't. And why should you? I don't know how to do your job! The art of research is in finding similar homes and adding value for benefits and reducing value for negatives.

Scoping out online resources

Online resources have exploded into the world of real estate in the last 10 years. In the very late '90s, web advertising companies approached my London agency boasting about the importance of an online presence. At that stage, not one sale in our office could have been linked to the internet in any form, so I told them politely that online presence was about as important as an open inspection at 6 am on a public holiday.

Now, only 10 years later, 95 per cent of buyers use the internet to find property.

We are now able to search for homes for sale virtually anywhere in the world. It seems incredible that from the comfort of our desks, we can see homes we're interested in buying from the sky, from the street, or in video format. We can see floor plans, photographs, get suburb details, see what has sold in that street for the last couple of decades, who paid what for it and when. We can have immediate online access to mortgage calculators, finance information, legal help, local council details, population information and the gender ratios in the area.

You should start your online research by learning about recent sales in the area in which you wish to buy. This will give you a good understanding of the market, and an awareness of how much various types of property sell for in the area. Following are some great Australian websites that make an excellent starting point for your research:

- <www.rpdata.com>

- <www.pdslive.com.au>

- <www.myhousevalue.com.au>.

Be aware that these sites charge for accessing the information, but it can be worth paying for a subscription for the period in which you are searching.

Another approach is to look at current homes for sale in the area. This can be a good idea, as the values will certainly be up to date. However, because the figures represent anticipated sale prices rather than actual sale prices, they will be less accurate than the statistics that you'll find relating to houses that have already sold.

In Australia, there are a number of main property portals that, when viewed together, combine virtually every home for sale in all areas. Some good ones are:

- <www.domain.com.au>

- <www.realestate.com.au>

- <www.homehound.com.au>.

Always check all three portals wherever you are looking, as some agents only list on one site.

There are also a number of websites that allow sellers to market their homes directly, rather than going through an agent. Examples of such websites are:

📷 <www.buymyplace.com.au>

📷 <www.buyitprivately.com.au>

📷 <www.propertyeasy.com.au>.

Chatting to local agents

Due to the historical element of online search engines, you should combine your online research with local knowledge. No-one is better placed to help you with up-to-date local know-ledge than the agents working in the area. Remember, agents only make money when you buy through them or sell your home with them, so if you want them to give you some free advice, you need to convince them that you are indeed planning to buy from them. Tell them what you want, and ask the agent whether your wishlist is realistic considering your budget. Also, ask them how often similar listings become available, and what is on offer now. Please remember that helpful agent when you do buy—we all have to make a living you know!

Don't forget the print media

Don't forget to check the property section of your local news-paper, or the free magazines available from your local agent's office. Because you have to set your criteria when searching online, some great homes could slip between the cracks of your search. Printed advertisements could expose a new location or type of home that you had not thought of before.

Understand your goals

Before you make an offer on a home, ensure you have a good idea of what winning actually means to you. For some, it's all about getting a bargain;

for others, it's a chance to get the home they really want — fair and square. Your answer to the question of what you want out of winning will affect the way in which you go about offering or bidding for your new house. Why? Because buying a home that is perfect for you should mean that you are prepared to pay a fair price, maybe even full asking price. It is worth it for the increase in the quality of life you and your family will experience as a result. But if you are buying a modest unit to use for long-term investment, you may just walk away if the price gets too high.

How to buy your home

Having found your dream home, it's down to the tricky part: learning about the various buying methods you might need to utilise in order to purchase your property. This will ensure that you don't get discouraged from securing what could be your ideal purchase purely because of the sale method.

There are three main ways to acquire a residential property in Australia—excluding befriending an elderly wealthy person and claiming to be their long-lost relative from Dubbo, of course. The following advice can only be a general guide, as specific regulations and conventions vary from state to state.

Private treaty

The term 'private treaty' is a rather grand and formal title for what is generally considered to be quite a normal method of selling property—but calling it the 'normal' method is rather unexciting, so private treaty it remains.

A private treaty involves a property being listed on the market by a seller or agent, usually with a stated price and no set deadlines for sale. The listing invites all prospective buyers to submit an offer in any form they choose, outlining their own conditions and dates. Most properties are sold this way. Quite often when an auction fails, a home will be put on the market in this form. For buyers it is the most straightforward, flexible and least intimidating form of sale, and most of them love its simplicity.

Once you have submitted your offer, the seller will respond. You might have to make another offer, to which the seller responds again and the negotiations continue.

Of course, the disadvantage from a buyer's point of view is the lack of urgency sometimes encountered—sellers can take long periods of time to respond to offers, meaning that other buyers have a chance to submit their offer. You find yourself part of a mini auction as sellers and agents play buyers against each other. It is possible in a good sellers' market for buyers to be messed around—and, I can assure you, this does happen. Before you start to moan (or have a voodoo doll made to look like the agent or seller), you must put yourself in the seller's place: if it were you, would you honestly refuse to listen to a potentially higher offer?

Winning a private treaty

Once you have selected a particular home, it's time to put your research to good use. Prior to choosing a particular home, you should have a feel of house values in the area, and a general view of what the market in the area looks like. So, let's say the home you like is listed at $400000. What should you do? Should you pay that price, or should you offer higher or lower?

You might have done some research and noted that the online property sites list homes similar to the one you're interested in for around $350000. Since the one you are considering is listed at $400000, you might be tempted to bid lower, which would be a smart move in most situations. But a low bid might not work if that house is the only one of its type for sale and you know the open inspections have been packed. In that situation, the seller may be pushing it by asking for $400000, but going as low as $350000 might lose you the sale. If you are well informed and use your common sense, you should have no trouble negotiating a scenario like this.

Tender

Buying a property by tender is probably the least utilised of the three processes. In my experience, tender is actually the only sale method that really establishes an accurate sale value (although in reality, most sellers don't want true value — they want more).

Tender can take various forms. As a general rule, selling a house by tender is in some ways similar to the private treaty method. It involves listing a home and inviting offers from prospective buyers. The main difference between tender and private treaty is the time constraint placed on buyers, who are invited to submit an offer to the seller, expressing their terms and conditions, by a stated set date. The idea behind this scenario is to place buyers under a form of date constraint. Buyers therefore have the opportunity to analyse the property and express exactly what it is worth to them. The figure they come up with is the true value of the property because it is not influenced by the hysteria of an auction environment, or the conventions involved in the private treaty method, where buyers offer a low initial figure as a way of negotiating a lower price. Other property professionals may not agree that sale by tender discloses the true value of a property, but don't worry about them — they are wrong!

There are of course pros and cons to this approach. As the buyer, you will have time to investigate the purchase before the set date, as it is unlikely that offers will be accepted prior to the set date. I say unlikely because conditions vary from state to state and also from seller to seller, but it is rare. Another advantage for you as the buyer is that you will know in a fairly short period of time whether you have secured the purchase, rather than having to wait for the seller to take six weeks to decide on each and every offer received. Also, if you offer what you are prepared to pay, you don't run the risk of getting carried away at auction or being forced up by other parties in a private treaty.

But the tender method can be a bit of a minefield. You'll have to involve yourself in some careful and detailed thinking to ensure your offer and terms are good enough to get the seller's attention without bidding more than you mean to. What makes this especially tricky is that as a buyer, you have no clue what other parties have offered to the seller — or even whether any other parties are interested at all. It really is a blind secret auction in its simplest form. So you have to decide what price level you are prepared to set, as you could end up offering considerably more (or less) than your competition.

Winning a tender

Winning in the tender situation requires a unique skill, because you don't know your competition. You may not know the other interested parties, or even whether anybody else is slightly tempted. But there are a few things you can do to gauge the interest in the house. For example, you could attend the open inspections and count the number of people that show up. (Never feel you shouldn't listen to other people's conversations in these circumstances — try hiding behind doors, or in cupboards.) Also, don't be afraid to push the agent: sometimes they might let out some valuable snippet of information on the property's price, the sellers or even the bottom line. Schmoozing with the agent is always a valuable activity: don't underestimate the power of a large skinny cappuccino and a blueberry muffin in winning them over. And no matter how painful you might find the agent to be, always act as if you love them.

The decision the seller makes to accept an offer is not always entirely about the monetary value of the offer. Favourable terms that the seller will like can also play a part, such as a quick settlement date or increased deposit size.

So although buyers can be scared away from this method, I would not worry — tender can be a very fair process.

Auction

An auction is a public sale where buyers bid against each other to buy a property. If the highest bid is acceptable to the seller, a sale occurs on the fall of the hammer. The highest bidder signs the contract and pays the deposit at the end of the auction.

Auction is a hugely popular method of sale in Australia, but I often encounter buyers who are actually dissuaded from even inspecting a home offered for auction because they are scared and intimidated by how stressful and unpredictable such a method of buying can be. Their fear relates to the auction itself. This is understandable, as there are many elements of the auction process that make it seem intimidating. However, as I will explain, there are steps you can take to ensure that you approach auctions with confidence, and with a bit of luck, come out with a win.

The auction process is governed by a variety of regulations and conditions, which of course vary from state to state (which is ridiculous—it should be the same everywhere—but don't get me started on that!). Usually, prospective buyers bid against one another to ascertain who will be prepared to pay the highest price. The highest bidder is announced by the auctioneer, and the sale of the property to that person is confirmed by the fall of a hammer. Generally, once this has happened, the property belongs exclusively to the highest bidder, who then has a previously stated number of days to settle. The buyer then pays his or her deposit and is contractually obliged to buy the home.

Sales contracts

A sales contract can be an extremely complex and lengthy document, which can intimidate buyers because of the confusing language it contains. In reality, most of the information in the contract will be pretty standard stuff. Work with your lawyer to ensure that you complete the contracts correctly, and that you are getting what you want in the arrangement. Specific things to check are:

▲ Is the price agreed correct?

▲ Are the settlement dates, deposit due dates, building inspection deadlines and payment schedules as expected?

Sales contracts *(cont'd)*

▲   What are stated penalties and when do they apply?

▲   Are all details as agreed?

▲   Is the home being sold with the inclusions you expected?

▲   Can you fulfil all the obligations stated in the contract?

Ask your lawyer to explain any part of the contract that you don't understand before you sign.

The majority of Australian property auctions don't include a price guide in their listings, a practice I personally find about as useful as an overseas call centre. In the odd but gloriously helpful occasion that price guides *are* stated, they are often much lower than the actual price to get you excited. This is fair enough — it is a sensible sales technique. I will have a moan about that later, but for now all you need to know is that the auction process is open by its very nature.

If you are interested in an online listing that has no price guide, there is a trick that could disclose the price of the home. Try performing a search for the house using several different price bands. Keep narrowing your range until the home appears as the only search result. The agent will have had to show a price search to submit the home to the website. This cannot always be accurate, but it might give you a clue!

Auctions can be unpredictable. Sometimes they can just come to a halt mid flow, usually because the home has not reached a certain value level. Alternatively, the auctioneer may disappear to 'take instructions' from his or her client, which basically signals a heated conversation between the agent and the disillusioned seller — the seller wants more money, the agent knows it is not happening and desperately wants to wrap up the deal and invoice his or her commission. The auctioneer will then skip back to the waiting masses (or the three prospective buyers and five neighbours who have turned up because the footy won't be on until later that day). He or she will then announce whether the home has reached a reserve price (the minimum price acceptable to the seller). This is often when the *real* negotiations begin. Because the reserve has been reached, people get a little excited because a sale is about to happen, and may bid more emotionally than they did before. Alternatively, when the reserve price has not been made, the auctioneer will invite the last bidder to come and have a chat with the sellers to try and seal the deal. The unpredictable nature of an auction environment means that all your research needs to be undertaken prior to auction day.

The seller will be desperately hoping that two potential buyers will be carried away in a bidding war that will elevate the final sale price beyond expectation—and that can happen, so watch out. If the hammer falls, you are committed: no excuses. Even if you submit an offer in the 'discreet room' that is often located at the rear of the building (to ensure privacy for the seller and prospective buyer), you may find you are bound by auction conditions, so check beforehand. If you are in that discreet room and seem to be the only buyer there, play hard to get—check that the conditions meet *your* expectations. Oh the joy of power!

Bidding before the auction begins

If you are really desperate to secure a home, you can always submit an offer prior to auction. Of course, sellers are not obliged to accept your offer, but it may be worth a try. Don't worry if the 'will sell prior to auction' statement is not advertised — we do live in a free market. That said, do always remember that winners can be losers: the bidder who secured the property but paid way too much for it because he got involved in a personal bidding war with the guy at the back with the tattoos and dark glasses might end up in a right financial mess just because he wanted to win.

Winning at auction

Tactics for winning at auctions are a hotly debated topic. I hate to be the bearer of bad news, but unfortunately, there is no secret winning formula for success as a buyer at auction. This is because to win, you must be able to read the auction room and adapt your actions and tactics to the scenario. So any tactic will depend on the specific situation.

For example, a popular piece of advice given to prospective homebuyers is to be strict about the figure you set. But this advice will depend on whether your situation demands it. For example, perhaps the maximum amount available to you is $300000, and that includes selling your V8 ute, your favourite surf board and your body to anyone that will have it. In this case, even $1 will be too much more and you would do well to adhere to the rule. However, there are times where you may have a little more financial flexibility. In this case, you might have set a maximum of $300000 knowing you have a little more to play with. In some instances, playing a 'shock bid' (for example, bidding $20000 more than the last bid) shuts the room up, and the other potential buyers will drop away fearing you will take it all the way. In other cases, this can backfire and send the price spiralling higher even more quickly.

Andrew's **hot tip**

Familiarise yourself with the process by attending a few auctions before you are ready to buy in order to get yourself comfortable with the rather strange world of the property auction.

Some only submit their first bid as the hammer is about to fall, a tactic used by many to ensure they don't push up the price too early in the proceeding. This technique can scare off the last bidder who thought a second ago that he or she had secured the home!

It is also possible to appoint someone to act on your behalf instead of attending the auction yourself—this may reduce the understandable pressure you might feel attending the auction. Check with a lawyer in your state to clarify this process.

> ### Don't forget the research!
>
> The secret of winning at an auction is to know what you're getting involved in: the more knowledge you have of the auction process, the property itself and the market, the more chance you have of buying a house you love at a price you're happy with. Before you go to the auction, you should become very familiar with the following things:
>
> ▲ the current housing market in the area you're looking (as you should in every type of buying situation)
>
> ▲ every detail of the property itself, including specifications and location.
>
> With a good knowledge of the housing market in your area and a solid understanding of the property itself, you'll be in a good position to judge what sellers and other buyers are playing at on the day of the auction. This should allow you to have a realistic perception of the environment in which you're operating. Of course, many others will be doing exactly the same thing to you, so it is all fun and games really.

How to handle defeat

The trouble with property deals is the sheer amount of dollars on the line. It is very easy to get emotional and stressed as a result of the huge commitment you will be making. This is exacerbated by the fact that homes or blocks are almost never available in their exact identical form elsewhere—because if they were elsewhere they wouldn't be identical. Follow me? So, it's easy to find yourself becoming emotionally attached to the idea of buying *that particular house.*

This is precisely why you should be conscious that defeat is possible. I would be the first person to admit that this is so very hard to do, especially when you have found that perfect property. It could have taken you months of searching to find it, and you may have had countless sleepless nights where you dreamed of showing off your new purchase to your mates. You have even begged your boss for a raise or sold your children (that is a joke, by the way) because you wanted the house so much. (P.S. I don't expect homebuyers to start selling children—that would make no sense. Most kids wouldn't even raise sufficient funds to cover the building and pest inspection! Joking again, get back in your box.)

Obviously, the thought of potential defeat is not the right frame of mind to start negotiating with a potential seller, but sometimes an obsession with a particular property can make you vulnerable. This can lead you to become blind and pay too much for the home, or worse: failing to pay full attention to what you are actually buying and missing the tell-tale signs of problems that could relate to the structure of the house, the block or the location.

I would hate to stop buyers getting enthusiastic—as you all know, I can get carried away with a lovely property opportunity within seconds of walking over the boundary. But I know the risk of losing your mind over the perfect property, so I urge you to enjoy the excitement, but combine it with a certain amount of realism.

Don't let this sale method scare you away from a home you really like. The reality is that auctions don't have to be intimidating, and hopefully by reading this book you will feel a lot more confident about them.

. . . .

What's the agent thinking?

When agents show you around a home, you may try to tailor what you say and how you react to convey a message to the agent. But in many cases, the agent can see right through you.

You say: 'What a great home! I will definitely get my partner to come and look at it during the week'.

Agent thinks: *You hate the place and cannot wait to get out of here.*

You say: 'This isn't bad—we might consider it, if the price is right, but we are not that fussed'.

Agent thinks: *Whoa, they love it. I don't care what offer they give me, I have to get this one over the line!*

Ugly duckling or swan?

Chapter 3

Deciding whether a renovation project is for you

To buy a gorgeous home, or to buy a tip? I learned very early on in my real estate career that I loved buying the ugly ducklings. I mean, I always dreamed of buying gorgeous 'finished' homes, but in about 80 per cent of my property purchases, I ended up with the renovation project.

So is there a magic formula that determines what kind of property you should buy and under what circumstances? Like everything in property, there is no clear-cut answer—all I can do is give you some clues to help decide what type of buyer you are.

My love of 'housing horrors' has led me to purchase some glowing examples of ugly ducklings.

My first home, as explained in chapter 1, could only be described as a disgusting, filthy tip. The scary thing is that it was this tip-like quality that attracted me to it. My house was only 10 years old at the time, and architecturally boring. But then, so were all the homes in that suburb, so I thought I could simply redecorate it and refit the kitchen and bathroom, after which it would be perfectly adequate. I could see its potential very easily.

I once bought a 100-year-old cottage that was perched precariously on the side of a cliff. Not only had the cottage not been modernised for 40 years, but someone had died in it! The walls holding the cottage back from the cliff were, shall we say, decidedly wonky. In addition, the vehicle access to the property was so limited and narrow that the small truck delivering the kitchen made the local press when it got stuck around a corner, its underside caught on the slope. It had become a sort of truck seesaw, with none of its wheels touching the narrow old street. Within months of moving into this historical dream home, the drains collapsed and my lucky neighbour had the benefit of waste seeping into her kitchen slab floor—nice!

This was followed by another stone cottage, this time 150 years old, which had been owned by a single family for generations. On walking through the door of this house, you literally fell through the floor, which was held together by the old lino laid on the floor's surface. As a bonus, the house did have an internal toilet, but that was under the stairs. Also, apparently people were more compact 150 years ago than they are now, because despite not being the world's tallest person myself, I would spend half my time knocking my head on the architraves. On one occasion while renovating the cottage, I decided to burn all the debris that was piling up in the garden to avoid expensive refuse removal costs. All went well until the heat of the fire reached the base of the bonfire, which contained the lino floor. It had been the first item stripped out, and was made of pure linseed oil—oh my God did it burn and burn, to the point where I nearly had no cottage left!

It did clear the rubbish though.

My list of housing horrors carried on well through my twenties and into my early thirties. When I first met my wife, I had just bought a new home—well, not *new*, of course, but an old warehouse unit that had been converted 20 years before. And now it needed—guess what?—a full reno! During our courtship, the majority of the entertaining that my wife-to-be and I did together was at her place. It was during this time that I learned that women are not quite as accepting as men are of living in total squalor and mess, but I loved it. It was easier than doing the housework and you had the ultimate excuse for being lazy—why clean up when the house is constantly dirty because of the renovations? So, rather than cleaning up after the daily builder's visits in order to impress my wife-to-be, I moved in with her. Clever, eh?

After a few months of living in my new lady's house, we decided to move back into my soon-to-be-completed warehouse conversion and rent her home out to tenants. We secured a tenant and went on holidays, having been assured by the man in charge of my renovation that the works would be completed by the time we came back. The only problem was: he got the date wrong! We had just flown back from Australia, and had arrived back to a grey, gloomy and cold London day, totally jet-lagged and with desperate dreams of a comfortable bed. When we opened the door, we were greeted by a half-completed building site! As for the beds, well, they were still dismantled, stacked in corners and surrounded by boxes. This was certainly not what my lovely new partner really had in mind, and somehow she did not seem to relish the idea of sleeping on a dusty mattress in a kitchen—women are such odd creatures!

You would have thought that this experience would have sig-nalled the end of my desire to buy homes that needed work, but no! And my new wife seemed to be of the same inclination—just less flexible on the sleeping-on-a-dusty-mattress bit!

So we carried on moving and putting ourselves through the hell of living mid reno. Over the years, we grew accustomed to it: we learned to live with having hardly any working power sockets, only one working toilet (when the water was on, that is!), and a single operational bath or shower with water pressure more like a drizzle than a tropical storm! Oh, and we soon got used to the kitchen resembling a campsite—who needs bench tops and running water? It all sounds fine to me!

The biggest shock of my life was after my family and I hit Australian shores. I really did believe that my desire to renovate had finally burnt out, and so did my wife and kids. But no, our new Australian family home was to be another renovation project. The kitchen had no dishwasher, but it did have an oven— only problem was that it needed to be turned on the day before you wanted to cook your turkey twizzlers to allow time for it to heat up to a whopping 50 degrees! The house had one working shower, hardly any wardrobe space, a lack of decent lighting and no power anywhere you needed it. Even the swimming pool was falling apart. The water tank leaked and the drains collapsed time and time again. Everything around us fell off, broke down or leaked—the pure delight of living in a renovation project!

So as you can see, there are negatives to taking on a renovation project, especially if it is a home you plan to live in. But I can see negatives with well-presented homes, too.

Whether or not to buy a 'swan'

When deciding whether or not to buy a new home, or a renovation project, it's important to think carefully about whether you have the time, energy, skills or inclination to undertake or supervise renovation works. The boxes on pages 44 to 45 and 49 to 50 outline the pros and cons of each option, and I'll go into more detail about each option later in the chapter.

Pros and cons: finished house

After reading my story, I am sure you are already working out the pros of buying a well-maintained house! Some of them are:

▲   What you see is what you get (that, of course, is the theory). It's therefore easier to make the decision to buy in the first place — either you like it or you don't.

▲ Renovated houses are easier to budget for. All you have to do is maintain the home, and any changes you might want to make are likely to be affordable rather than having to beg your lender for more money.

▲ It means an easy life! Spend your spare time going out, entertaining and showing off your new purchase rather than slaving away on home improvements.

▲ It's easier to raise finance on the new home, as the lender or valuer can see exactly what they are risking their money on.

▲ It's a great choice for people who think 'tools' are a function on your computer!

There are, of course, cons to buying a sparkling new or a perfectly presented home. Some of these are:

▲ You pay more for a finished house because someone else has already done the work for you.

▲ You must make sure the fittings and the style of the home are exactly to your taste. The biggest mistake you could make would be to pay top dollar for a well-presented home and then want to change the kitchen, tiles or bathrooms.

▲ Well-presented or staged homes usually generate more buyer interest, so you could find yourself in strong competition with other buyers. This could jack up the price.

▲ Any changes you make will not necessarily add value in the short term. If you own the home for five to 10 years, you will still have to update it when you come to sell.

All that glistens isn't necessarily gold: buying a renovated house

It is easy for prospective buyers to get confused and misled when they instantly fall in love with a gorgeous house. This experience happens most frequently when inspecting a well-presented home that is few years old. Sometimes this gut feeling is correct, but sometimes you'll find that you've been fooled by excellent presentation and a few old selling tricks, and your dream home isn't everything it's cracked up to be. To avoid spending a lot of money on something that is not really worth it, you need to know how to look through that 'perfect presentation'.

As a huge fan and expert of 'home staging', as we agents call it, I do not want to encourage you to look through *all* the staging— or a whole element of my expertise will be compromised! However, I will let you in on a few secrets, providing that you keep the information under your hat.

Whether you are inspecting a renovated old home or a beautifully furnished modern home, as a buyer trying to decide whether to commit to one of these shining examples of dreamy lifestyle you must always ask the following four questions about the house's features:

- What will it look like after the sellers and their expensive furniture have moved out and the home is an empty void?

- Is this really a sensible price, or am I getting carried away?

- Will it date?

- Will it depreciate?

I'll discuss these issues individually to help you negotiate your way through the mysterious world of househunting in Australia.

What will it look like after the sellers move out?

When inspecting a well-presented home, it's very important to try to visualise what the rooms will look like when the current owners move out. It might seem obvious, but most of the things that you love about the house won't be there when the owners move out—they may have been placed strategically to make every square metre of the home look great. Fittings are generally included because they are secured to the structure of the house. The first of these points is actually quite easy to address. Kitchen fittings are always included, but check that all those chic appliances that enhance that space so very well are actually included.

If they are not, demand they are! Bathrooms—nice easy one, all included.

But anything that can be easily removed might not be included, so watch out. That can include:

- furniture
- appliances such as microwaves and dishwashers
- light fittings
- window dressings
- rugs
- planters
- kids' outdoor play equipment
- outdoor furnishings.

Not only do you need to check exactly what is staying, but you should ask yourself whether you like the majority of the fittings *in situ,* and whether the decor style and colours will work with your furnishings. If you are starting out, that is not a worry, but if you have spent thousands of dollars on furniture already, it's important to be sure that your existing items match the decor.

Chattels

The seller can decide what's included in the sale of their property, and the statement 'what you see is what you get' might not necessarily apply. Sellers can specify in the contract if they want to take any fittings or extras that buyers may think are included. This is not an opportunity for a seller to strip the home bare, but common chattels not included in a sale include window dressings, light fittings and some appliances. If any of these items are important to you as a seller, you must state their exclusion or put a price on them remaining. If you are in love with a beautiful stone bench in the backyard, and it suddenly isn't there on the moving day, check if it was an exception to items included in the chattels, because, if it was, then you've got no leg to stand on, as well as no bench to sit on.

Is the price sensible?

It may surprise you, but I have witnessed so many buyers lose their ideal purchase because of price. Contrary to what others may tell you, it can be a bad idea to get hung up on every dollar. If the home is perfect for you, you are likely to stay there a long time. The fact that you love the whole space means that the costs of changes will be minimal, and you will not have the expense of moving again in the near future because the home is right for you.

Buyers often fall in love with a house, but the price is a bit heavy. The buyer then gets all wrapped up in negotiations until they are $5000 away from securing the deal. Still they will not budge. Of course, it can be argued that the sellers are being stubborn — well, they *are*. But if you were in their situation, you may be too. If the home works for you in every way and you have researched and completed your homework, that extra $5000 or $10000 in a period of five years or more will soon be forgotten. Regretting not securing your dream home will be remembered for a long period of time, and your partner is likely to remind you of it constantly. Of course, you should not go mad and offer ridiculously high figures — it is all about careful thought and the confidence that this is the right home for you.

Will it date?

Will it date? Of course it will. 'Dating' relates to the aesthetics of a property's fittings and specifications — it is purely a style and personal taste issue. So whether or not something will date is not so much a question of *if* it will date, but rather *how long* it will stay trendy. You need to realise that your perfect home will not only look a little worn in five years, but in 10 years' time it will look out of date. Some features will date more quickly than others. They are very hard to list, but the rule of thumb is this: if a feature has been around for a long time and seems to feature everywhere you look, it may be getting close to the end of its fashion cycle. Interiors, thank goodness, have more longevity than clothes.

Will it depreciate?

Depreciation is a reduction in value over time. Again, the answer to the question of depreciation is 'Yes, it will depreciate'. Obviously, a new kitchen is no longer new in five years. However, what is less obvious is the fact that you need to ensure that the fittings have an overall appeal rather than an appeal that is specific to your tastes (because you are the only buyer that actually loves their purple kitchen). Brightly painted walls are no problem because they're easy and cheap to change. But very personal selections of tiling or kitchen fittings can be expensive to change if they don't have mass buyer appeal—so never pay top dollar for personalised fittings, even if they match your style and taste. The only exception to this is when you can be certain you will not be selling for many years.

Buying a dump: pros and cons

Having read the cons of buying a finished house, I expect many of you are thinking that you could happily tackle a renovation project, despite my frank and honest potted personal history. I can assure you that most of you could not. People who are looking to buy in suburbs where older homes feature often say things such as: 'We don't mind a bit of work'. This is usually a lie. When it comes down to actually living with a project, it is not exactly a fairy tale—although admittedly there are some benefits.

 Pros and cons: renovation projects

Some positive elements of buying a renovation project are:

▲   Unrenovated homes offer value for money.

▲   You could have the chance to buy in a street or suburb that would normally be out of your price range.

Pros and cons *(cont'd)*: **renovation projects**

▲ You are free to renovate the property to exactly your taste and style.

▲ You'll get plenty of satisfaction from completing the project to the admiration of friends and family (this one may seem ridiculous but it is true).

And here are some of the cons:

▲ Paying too much for renovations. The cost of your works plus your purchase price should never equate to more than the house's future renovated value.

▲ Controlling your style and taste and adapting for your suburb's market.

▲ Living in what will probably be little more than a building site, for months and months (sometimes years!) watching the budget run out, your marriage fail and your children leave home care of social services.

▲ Securing contractors, adhering to budgets and losing all your spare time to weekends constantly spent at Bunnings and IKEA.

Am I *really* ready to take on a renovation project?

Along with the issues discussed in the boxes previously, there are some key elements of your life that will be affected by your choice to buy an ugly duckling.

Are you ready for a lifestyle change?

Never underestimate the effect your decision will have on your lifestyle. Whether you are buying as a single person, a couple or a family, you should keep in mind that even the *managing* of a project that you've outsourced to others could be time-consuming. Look at how you spend your time: do you honestly have room in your life for such a project? If sports or other hobbies fill your week already, maybe it is not the option for you at this point of your life.

What's your level of DIY ability?

Even a modern home that only requires minor enhancement will involve certain skills and some work on your part to avoid going over budget. Whether you are male, female or in between, if you are filled with dread at the thought of clearing rubbish, ripping out kitchens and bathrooms, stripping paintwork, clearing yards, spending hours in building supply stores, loading and unloading utes and painting and cleaning, then this may not be the option for you. But if you have a talent or practical skill that could contribute to your ability to undertake some of the work (or you have mates or family that do), it might be worth considering. Just be honest with yourself, because buying a property requiring work when you had planned to do no more than sign the contract, puff up a few cushions and choose which shade of taupe to paint the lounge room is not going to work.

What are your priorities?

Even if a home is a bargain and you know you could make a profit after renovating, a decision to buy a renovation project is a big one and you need to make sure you are willing to make the home your first priority. Most of you actually have a life outside of houses—I never did, so renovating was always my priority, but I was weird. Never underestimate how much a renovation project will take over your life. If you really do not have your heart and soul in the project and you run out of drive halfway through, not only will your partner and family suddenly demand that you complete the job, but you will not have a get-out clause. The home will be left half finished, and could actually be worth less than you paid for it!

I'm ready! I want a renovator's delight!

As a buyer of a renovator's delight, you need to consider all the issues. I say 'issues' because problems may arise from factors that don't include the state of the kitchen and bathrooms. There may be structural defects, major floor plan issues or awful decoration—overgrown yards or just a really filthy, smelly interior. These are discussed following.

See through the mess to the potential

If you are able to mentally strip the building back, you are one step ahead of the crowd. Mentally stripping a room back to its foundations can be a difficult talent to master, but it's a skill that will serve you well.

So how can you do this?

You need to be able to visualise a fully furnished, possibly untidy, room totally empty. Then, you need to project your dream interior into it. Use the following method:

1   Stand in any room of the house and imagine it totally empty.

2   If it is painted in strong colours, wall papered or covered in pictures or posters strip it back in your mind to a blank, plain white space.

3   The final part is imagining it newly furnished and modernised. Perhaps have a list of the changes you plan to make as you undertake this rather strange process.

4   Always be honest with yourself. If you really can't imagine what the house would look like with your dream interior, get help!

Assess the amount of work involved

What will it cost to turn the decrepit building you've purchased into a pleasant dwelling you'd be happy to live in? I'm sorry to sound harsh, but the pure and simple fact is that if you are a first-time renovator who has no links to the building industry and no personal experience or expertise, you don't have a clue. This should not stop you, but you should be prepared to seek help and advice and be realistic about the time and money you're investing.

If you come across a home that needs work and decide you like it, you should book another inspection at your convenience and warn the agent/seller you will be there a while — maybe an hour or so. Ask if they will let you take photos — not all agents will oblige, but try.

Arrive at the second inspection with any experts you feel you need to assist you to make an accurate assessment of the situation. Carefully inspect both the inside and outside of the house, and make careful notes about everything you will need to fix or alter to bring the house up to the standards you are envisaging.

Outside

Take careful note of the condition of the outside of the house, as well as any other structural or aesthetic flaws you think will need attention. Ask for professional assistance where possible. Things to watch out for include:

- *Roof.* Step back from the building and look at the roof. Ask yourself the following questions:

    □ Are the guttering and downpipes all intact?

    □ Are tiles in good condition?

    □ Is the roofline straight, or is it sagging?

    □ Does it look like a big rainstorm would be kept at bay?

- *Walls.* These need to be straight and look like they can fight off rain and wind. Check the ground levels. If they are too high (over the slab height) our little chums the termites could find a way in, and so could moisture.

- *Windows.* When looking at windows, ensure that the glass is not broken and that they open and close smoothly. Ask yourself the following questions:

    □ Do the windows need to be replaced?

    □ Does their style suit the building?

- *Fences.* Ensure that all boundaries are clearly marked and fenced. Ask yourself whether the fences are in good or bad condition. If the property has retaining walls, check their condition. These are very costly to correct, and add absolutely no value because buyers expect them to be good.

- *Garages and outbuildings.* External structures are second in importance to the main building of course, but still worth a check if their usage is going to be important to you.

- *Garden.* It is usually very obvious if things need to be done in the garden, but always include the costs of potential landscaping in your renovation budget.

 Don't forget to check modern-day essentials such as broadband access!

Inside

Look at the following things inside the house; again, seek professional advice where possible:

- *Walls.* Ensure all walls are in good condition. You should ask yourself the following questions:

  □ Are the walls straight?

  □ Are there cracks?

  □ Do any surfaces appear to be in poor condition?

  □ Are they feeling damp, or showing signs of moisture damage?

- *Ceilings.* Check to see if the ceilings are in good condition. Check the following things:

  □ Are there obvious signs of water damage?

  □ Are there any cracks in the ceiling, cornicing or light fittings?

- *Floors.* The floor itself should feel stable and strong, and you should check what is underneath the main flooring.

- *Fittings.* Look closely at all kitchen fittings. You should specifically check the following:

  □ Are doors and drawers working well? Look for chips and cracks.

  □ Do the appliances work, and how clean are they?

- *Power supply.* You should spend some time ensuring that all the power supplies are working satisfactorily. Check the following things:

  □ Look at the main electrical switchboard. Is the wiring tidy and clearly labelled?

  □ How many power outlets are there in each room?

  □ Do points and lights all work?

- *Water pressure.* Locate the pump, and check the hot water system. Remember to try taps and showers.

- *Hidden areas.* Look in all cupboards, wardrobes, cellars and attics to establish that all these areas are clean and safe.

Take it all in! Take your time, and take plenty of notes. You'll need an accurate reference guide for the next phase of the operation.

Andrew's hot tip

Remember, many serious faults are hidden, such as termite infestation and structural faults. If you have any suspicions whatsoever, get a structural engineer in to look over your property — if serious faults are found, the seller may drop the price substantially. Even if you learn that you can't afford to pay for the home and the repairs it needs, it is worth spending the money on the research; the cost of the research will be a lot less than the cost of having to fix hidden structural defects!

The true cost of renovating

If you have decided that you are ready and able to undertake a renovation project, you need to create a quick but pretty damn accurate renovation budget. Your budget needs to cover everything—and I mean *everything*—because failure to come up with an accurate budget is where many buyers fail to make a single cent. The reason the budget has to include the lot is to comply with one very clear rule: your budget should not exceed the difference between the purchase price and the end value.

Andrew's hot tip

There are always exceptions to the rule that renovation adds value. For example, very old homes that are sold unmodernised can have added value because they contain appealing period details. In such an instance, you can actually reduce its status in the marketplace with too many architectural changes.

Working out your end value

In order to work out the end value, it's important to do your research (see chapter 10) so you know the market well enough to make an accurate decision. Remember to base the home's renovated value on the market as it stands rather than guessing its value in the future.

You should always build in a little extra to cover a slight downturn in the home's value, and ensure you can still afford to hold on until values rise again. I illustrate how a property downturn can affect renovation projects in the example below.

Finishing renovations

It's important to allow some money in your budget for a downturn in the property market. For example, let's say you have a budget of $350 000. You find a home selling for $300 000, and estimate that it could be worth $350 000 fully modernised.

A year later, having done some renovations, you reassess your budget, only to discover that you have spent $28 000 and think you need a further $10 000 to complete the renovation. Unfortunately, at this point you decide to sell because your funds are running out.

The market has not moved since you bought the house, and on getting the home re-valued, you are shocked to discover that the current value of your home has only increased to $320 000.

This occurs because people forget that until a home is virtually 100 per cent completed, the renovation costs and profit are rarely recovered in a sale. I have seen many occasions where an unfinished project sells for less than its original sale price! So before you purchase a 'renovator's delight', make sure you have the staying power to complete the renovation from start to finish.

Still not put off? Maybe you do have the staying power. I will remind you of my warning mid reno when you haven't had a normal kitchen or bathroom for four months, and the last time your entertained at home you were living in another home!

Creating a renovation brief

A useful tool when determining the amount you will need to spend on your renovation project is a renovation brief. This is a document that estimates the type of work that needs to be done and puts a monetary value on it. You will probably find yourself with very little time before purchasing to make a decision, and you are probably loathe to pay for any specialised reports and estimates at this stage, so a simple renovation brief is a relatively quick and accurate solution.

The purpose of this rough costing is to help you to evaluate the price you should consider offering. Often buyers see a renovator's delight advertised and think it must be a bargain. This might not be the case, so be aware and don't get too carried away.

During the process, obtain a floor plan. If one is not available through the seller, draw a rough one, measuring all rooms, windows and doors. Be sure to note power outlets. This plan will be invaluable in creating a good price guide for renovation costs. It will take very little time to obtain measurements and create a rough renovation brief, but the amount of money it will save you is potentially massive.

Ideally, you need to break the costing into sections (explained further in the following pages) because this will enable you to obtain verbal quotes from contractors or suppliers who could undertake the works more quickly and easily. It also helps to include as much information as possible in the brief, such as the materials you would like used, and the measurements of each room and element. This will encourage contractors to give a rough quote on the spot. If you give contractors enough information, they can give you a price guide without inspecting the home. But if you ask contractors 'how much to renovate my three-bedroom home?', they will look at you and then ask you if you are taking the proverbial.

Deciding what needs to be done

When determining what kind of work needs to be done on your house, remember that you don't have to do everything straight away—so it is often a good idea to divide your renovation brief into immediate and non-immediate categories. However, if you are planning to sell on straight away or to rent the home to tenants, all the works must be carried out immediately.

Essential works

Essential work refers to things that need to be done in order to make the house liveable, and includes anything that relates to the main fabric of the building. Ascertain exactly what you think needs to be installed and connected; again give contractors as much information as possible.

Essential work includes structural repairs such as:

- *Restumping.* If the home is on stumps, and these stumps are old or damaged, attend to them as a matter of priority or your investment could collapse—literally.

- 📠 *Repairing termite damage.* It is pointless to renovate your home until this problem is halted, because these little critters eat away at the structural components of the building. Often, the repairs are not as bad as they may seem.

- 📠 *Replacing roofing.* Roofs need to be water tight to avoid damage. Do not forget that guttering has to operate well, too—so make this a priority.

- 📠 *Fixing moisture penetration.* Water and moisture destroy buildings. To fix moisture damage, you'll need to stop water getting into cracks, mend leaking gutters and ensure no outside wall areas adjoin constant moisture points.

- 📠 *Check electricity outlets.* Our demand for power outlets at home has doubled in the past two decades, so ensure there are sufficient working power points in each room.

- 📠 *Check that gas is working.* Ensure the gas supply is in good working order, and repair it if necessary.

- 📠 *Repairing drainage.* Water damage stains can make buyers very nervous. Repair any damaged areas, ensuring you know you have solved the original problem that caused the damage.

- 📠 *Update or repair plumbing.* In much older homes, ensure that drains are working effectively, and that water supplies are all in good working order.

- 📠 *Fixing ceilings and wall surfaces.* My pet hate is an owner doing a huge amount of work on an old home, and then forgetting to finish the ceiling and wall surfaces to a high standard! Patching up is almost a total waste of time, so get the job done professionally: replaster, reline and resurface—it is worthwhile!

- 📠 *Replacing windows or doors.* These finishing items can transform your home from grotty to great! When replacing windows and doors, choose the style carefully—it will have a massive impact on the aesthetics of the home.

🏠 *Repair faulty air conditioning (if applicable).* Renovating
a dated home but leaving 20-year-old air conditioning
units is a no-no! If your budget is tight, just install new
fans—old units will totally date the whole home. If your
home is in a market where ducted systems are more
common, look at installing that type of system rather than
adding just new split systems. In an average home, two or
three new splits installed compared to the cost of a basic
ducted system are negligible and there is a real value and
saleability difference.

Non-essential works

Anything that does not relate to the main fabric of the building
or the fundamental liveability of the house can wait a while.
These include:

🏠 *Kitchen units.* If you don't have the budget to do a whole
kitchen makeover, new bench tops, appliances, doors
and handles can do the job. Make sure the layout works
for modern-day living. Check magazines and kitchen
showrooms for ideas.

🏠 *Bathroom fittings.* Although many people love the idea
of a brand-new bathroom that matches current decor
and fitting trends, if you avoid moving things around
drastically (shower, sinks, toilet), you will find it a lot easier
to stick to your budget.

🏠 *Lights.* Ensure the lighting makes the most of the decor.
Modern, attractive light fittings can really lift your home,
so be a bit creative here. A light supplier will be a great
source of inspiration and design advice.

🏠 *Flooring.* When renovating, follow the 'neutral' route when
it comes to flooring. This will ensure the flooring doesn't
date too quickly, and will increase future saleability. When
dealing with 'wet' areas (bathrooms, laundries) generally
use tiles. Kitchens should be tiled too, but as these areas
are often open plan, link the flooring visually to the rest

of the space. Living areas should be tiled or have wooden flooring to meet today's buyers' demands. Bedrooms and the formal lounge room should have carpet for comfort. Avoid dark colours if your home struggles for light, but try darker flooring if your home is bathed in Aussie sunshine and has light, neutral walls. Avoid patterns, tricky tile designs and edging—it may look great now, but how will it look in a few years when you want to re-sell?

- *Fencing.* If fencing or boundaries are in poor repair (or nonexistent), don't neglect them! Shabby fencing will stick out like a sore thumb, but if it looks great, it is the icing on the cake.

- *Driveways.* The driveway is the entrance to the home, so if it is ugly, unfinished or dated, it says all the wrong things about the home. So unless you live directly on a beach, do not ignore this factor.

- *Garages/carports.* The importance of external building structures depends on your home. For example, in an urban townhouse, even having space for a carport will be a bonus, so transformation to a garage won't be necessary. But if you live in a suburb where a double garage is the norm and you only have a carport, it's probably worth forking out for the double garage.

Make sure to note the specifications of the kitchen and bathroom in your brief. Take pictures to show suppliers, and know how many square metres you require of tiling, carpet and so on.

Cosmetic works

Anything that relates to the aesthetics of the house but doesn't affect the basic structure also can wait, and could even be carried out by you! This subset of renovation projects largely concerns the decoration of the house and may include:

- the painting (inside and out) of the house

- wall papering

- 🏠 landscaping (if applicable)
- 🏠 paving.

 Get to know material costs and typical daily rates for certain tradies so you can assess quotes rationally.

Establishing the cost of your proposed renovations

As you start to obtain quotes, be sure to keep in mind any talents you have, because the more you can do the more you can save. The biggest saving is always in the labour.

The final section of your brief should include all those little things often described as hidden costs. These can include:

- 🏠 *Council fees.* Any changes to the home's structure or layout may require approval from the local council or building control. You could be looking at many thousands in related fees, so keep this in mind when budgeting.

- 🏠 *Rubbish removal.* Debris created during the renovation needs to be packed up, loaded up and shipped out—this all costs money. Even a dumpster outside for a week is going to cost several hundred dollars, and you can fill one normally just by clearing the average overgrown backyard. Anything parked on a public road will need permission from our friends at the local council.

- 🏠 *Running costs during period of renovation.* If living off site during the renovations, you must budget for:
  - □ finance interest
  - □ insurance
  - □ rates
  - □ services.

🏠 *Professional services.* Architects and lawyers all charge, so factor in the cost of their services when doing a renovation budget.

If you plan to put in a whole new kitchen, it can help to have an idea of the cost of this project before you buy. Go to a supplier or show room with the floor plan you created at the start of the renovation project, and identify which specifications you'd like. Add this cost to your brief.

So armed with costing averages and a list of elements that need renovation, estimate the total renovation costs. The costs will comprise delivery, the material cost, labour costs and associated fees. A renovation brief will help you ascertain whether a home is worth renovating for profit, and how much you should consider paying for it. You'll often have limited time and be reluctant to spend money on accurate costing because you may not actually purchase the home. Get some average costings etched in your brain or logged on your laptop so you can use them. Your figures need to be conservative — no anticipation of special deals.

Green features

When deciding on specifications, it is a good idea to consider including 'green' features — and not just because reducing your environmental footprint will make you feel all warm and fuzzy. In most states, legislation dictates how you build a brand-new home in relation to 'green' features such as insulation, rainwater retention and energy-saving fittings. It is highly likely that further legislation will be introduced that requires energy efficiency ratings to be supplied for the sale of every established home — this is already happening in other countries. In the not-too-distant future, buyers will consider these ratings when deciding whether or not to purchase a house, and some ethically minded buyers may not even consider homes that don't have high ratings on the environmental front.

Once you secure the home

If you manage to secure the home, you'll need another budget, this time one that is seriously detailed. This time around, you have a lot more time to get it right, so don't rush the budget-making process!

Again, break all the elements down into sections like you did in your original renovation brief. Now you are at the start stage, your budget should include a work schedule. Many people fail to undertake works in the correct order. In fact, I've seen new ceilings get installed beautifully, and then the new owner decides she wants recessed lighting—too late now. I've seen owners complete inside works while the roof is still leaking.

Experts

If you are still absolutely determined to consider a renovation project, there are some people that can really help you: namely valuers, building inspectors and your local council.

Valuers

I have no idea why these guys are so underused by the buying public. I believe it is mainly because all your mates haven't bothered with valuers, so why would you?

Contact a valuer and ask them to value the home as it is, and then ask them what they think its potential value could be. Some valuers will even have a rough idea about how much it will cost you to renovate. They may not put their quote into writing, but they can make some agreeing or disagreeing noises when you mention a budget you have estimated.

It takes valuers years to gather their experience, and their findings are insurance backed. Importantly, they are totally independent and have no reason to make you buy or walk away—they are a buyer's natural ally.

Building inspectors

Track down good building and pest inspectors. Utilise a special-ist for each of these — that is, get a specialist building inspector and separate pest guy. Follow them around and ask questions. If they tell you that you need to replace six windows, you can ask, 'how much do you reckon, mate?' Detailed written quotes will cost you, but verbal guides may not.

Local council

If major changes are required, approach the local council and ask what they would expect to be involved in, and what charges you will have to pay them for the pleasure of their assistance. Also, ask them about the costs of the applications and the 379 forms that they will require you to complete in six languages, noting your shoe size on each.

Make a list of questions for which you need answers. Be precise and know your building. The more confident and direct you are, the more likely you are to get an honest and accurate response.

Do not forget helpful contractors — be nice, let them quote now for the real job. To the ones who could not be bothered say 'see ya'.

Who dares wins

The 'ugly duckling' can be a great purchase, as long as certain key elements have been thought through carefully. The following factors should be in place before you buy a renovation project:

- the price needs to be right
- your budget should be thorough and accurate
- your dedication needs to be real
- your research should be thorough
- your temperament needs to be tolerant.

Buying a home to renovate can make you a good profit, but never take this proposition for granted. Always build in a contingency fund and include *all* costs. Do the job well— complete it, and try not to be tempted by the purple kitchen. Importantly, never expect to make any money until you have finished, cleaned up, put up the new mail box and mowed the newly turfed lawn.

Similarly, a well-presented home can be a perfect buy—you avoid hours of planning and budgeting, and the months of sleeping on the floor among the rubble, and you can actually entertain friends and family rather than the endless tradies who arrive while you are still in the temporary shower room with no door. Buy perfection and lap it up! Again be certain that:

- you don't pay too much

- you love everything about the home and it's not just the dressings that makes the home.

What's the agent thinking?

Renovator's delights are pretty popular listings for agents. The fact they are perceived as a cheap deal or a chance to get into a good suburb for less means buyers love them, and agents know this. So watch out for remarks from agents such as: 'I doubt it will cost you that much to modernise, sir!' Or, 'I couldn't say exactly how much it will go for, of course, but I do need to let you know we have been literally inundated with prospective buyers on this one'.

Comments such as this are usually followed by a little smile.

As an agent, I too have been guilty of such tricks. Why? Because agents spend most of their time struggling to get prospective buyers through a normal home, and they struggle even more to get people excited when they do show up. So when the renovation project comes up and buyers start sniffing around in their masses, you can see the commission already. You cannot blame us, can you?

On many occasions, agents will send the junior staff or assistant to the inspections for ugly ducklings because they know such homes sell themselves. So if you get the new assistant or junior, please be nice — because the new agent will be nervously pacing and hoping no-one will ask awkward questions such as 'what zoning is the block?' or 'where was the historical termite damage and what remedy was used?' or 'has the council stated the specification for the re-stumping?' or, even worse, 'what were homes in this area selling for five years ago?'

At inspections for renovated homes, the agent might look nervous. This is not because he or she is new to the job or thinks you recognise him or her from your last trip to the local adult entertainment shop. It is because the agent's client is paranoid that no-one will scuff the timber floors, get dirt on the cream stair carpet, scratch the perfect walls or sit on a bed and ruin the setting before the buyers go through the room. You can always spot these agents: they always take their shoes off and walk around in socks and they follow your children around with a very careful, nervous eye. So for once, show a little sympathy please.

Agents love the perfectly presented listing, because it is a delight compared with the average slum we are expected to sell. We love the renovator, too. Why? Because buyers love the cheapest home in the street, and that means an easy sell for the agent!

Shiny and new

Chapter 4

Buying a new build

It's a wonderful feeling to walk into a sparkling new house. If you have ever bought a brand-new home, you'll know what I mean. Often the keys are handed straight over and you, the lucky buyer, have nothing more to do than jump with joy at the thought of moving into a house with no decoration needed, brand-new fittings, all appliances under warranty, shiny new flooring and no cleaning required. Not only do you get a great new home to hang out in, but you can make money too, when you eventually want to sell it.

That sounds too good to be true, doesn't it?

I have had great success with new builds; I attribute my success to favourable market conditions more so than the fact that I was dealing with new builds though!

During the mid '90s, I moved to London for work, and I bought a unit that was under construction at the time of purchase. The price was agreed in March. The following year in April (only 13 months later), I sold the unit for a 60 per cent capital gain. In current values, that would translate to a $400 000 home being bought last year and sold this year at $640 000. A shockingly good result!

Andrew's hot tip

Be aware that no two houses are ever exactly identical, so you shouldn't ever directly compare them. Before you disagree and tell me that you know of two identical homes next to each other in a housing development — you are wrong. One of the houses will be decorated well, and the other will not; and they would both have been purchased at different times for different prices. As a result, six months later, one house's owner will need to sell because the bank is knocking on his door, while the other will only want to sell because her home's value has increased and she wants to trade up. Identical houses in the marketplace do not actually exist.

At another stage of the property cycle, I bought another brand-new unit. I negotiated hard, ensured I was not paying too much and within five years it had achieved capital growth of 40 per cent, which was okay, but by the seventh year, the capital growth was back down to 25 per cent. Using the same fictional $400 000 Australian home bought seven years ago, in this scenario the home rose to $560 000 after five years. Not bad, eh? But by year seven, it was down to $490 000. I still made a profit, but what a difference between these two scenarios! Both were in the same city, but the market conditions made all the difference. These are the ups and downs of buying any real estate.

In the Australian housing market, these changes in the market are just as commonplace as they are in Europe. Your success will be linked to the timing of your purchase, and whether it has been made after a boom, before the next boom, in a steady market, or during a buyers' or sellers' market. There are no hard and fast rules in real estate, because it is impossible to control or even predict how the property market will behave over a prolonged period of time—and the world of new builds is no different. There are, however, a few things that you should consider when deciding whether a new build is the right option for you, or whether you'd be better off buying an established home.

Andrew's **hot tip**

New builds are easy to re-sell if the market is hot, because unless you have hideous taste, the home should still look good and can be easily prepared for the market, but selling for a profit in a buyers' market is another thing altogether.

New versus old

I know people who would only ever buy new. They love the feel of a brand-new home, and the whole process that comes with it. Conversely, I also know of many people for whom the mere mention of the word 'new' when associated with housing fills them with dread and horror. So which option is right for you?

Pros and cons of buying a new build

I have happily dipped my toes into all types of real estate, ranging from brand-new masterpieces to 200-year-old bombsites. To help you decide which option is right for you, I've listed some of the advantages and disadvantages of buying a brand-new house.

Some advantages of buying a new build are:

▲ the opportunity to have the latest designs and fittings

▲ you can design a home that's right for you (if you are building or buying from a plan)

▲ new homes are low maintenance

▲ a home that has everything all ready to use is easy to budget for, because you don't have to factor in improvements or renovations

Pros and cons of buying a new build *(cont'd)*

▲ you'll most likely live in a smart new street environment, especially if you buy in a housing estate

▲ there is more potential for greener living with insulation, water-saving fittings and energy-efficient installations.

There are also some disadvantages to buying a new build. Some of these are:

▲ There is often an oversupply of housing stock available in housing developments. This means that your chances of selling can be severely affected, because you have numerous new homes around you to compete with. This equates to lots of choice for buyers, so making top dollar on your home can be particularly difficult. Buying at the later stages of construction on an estate can mean less competition, but it also means the best blocks might already have been sold and land prices may have increased.

▲ Housing developments often have an oversupply of rental stock, because new estates are very popular with investors. This abundance of supply for your product could affect you if you are planning to rent the home out to tenants. This problem is often far worse in a new unit development that specialises in units or townhouses because these developments tend to get numerous homes completed at one time. Expect to have to compete with other owners for those tenants in that situation.

▲ Owner occupation may be lower in housing developments than in established locations, because housing developments are so popular with investors. This can mean less permanency for residents, so communities are slower to establish.

▲ There's a possibility that you'll have to contend with construction delays if the home you wish to buy has not been built yet.

▲ Your new living environment may be cluttered by continuing construction works if you buy in a housing development. There is nothing like being woken up at 5.30 am by the builders next door every Saturday morning to make you feel at home in your new house!

▲ The locations chosen by developers to build new housing are often underserviced by amenities. This can make everyday tasks such as commuting to work, shopping and accessing services more difficult, and houses will be less popular with potential tenants and future buyers.

▲ Buying the unknown is a risk with which some people are uncomfortable. If a suburb is new or developing, it is impossible to predict whether it will establish itself quickly (as the plans suggest), or whether it will be unestablished for another decade.

Ready-to-go or build-your-own?

Once you've decided that you want to buy new, you need to decide whether you want to buy a ready-to-live-in house or if you want to buy a block of land and build your own home from scratch. Both options are most commonly available on housing developments, which bring their own issues and considerations, as we'll discuss later.

Newly built homes

A new build is a recently constructed dwelling that has never been lived in before. If the home is within a housing development, it is likely that a developer has already designed all the different home types within a complex.

Housing developments

Housing developments are structured building developments of residential properties. They are often large building complexes or large areas of land that are bought up by a developer, who divides them into 'blocks' and sells them. These blocks can be sold either as blocks of land that a buyer can build a home on, or as 'house and land' packages, which include the land and a brand-new house.

If you are purchasing a home in a housing development, you will simply need to select the position of your house within the existing complex—the choice of size and floor plan will be restricted. In the search process, you should be able to inspect a sample house or unit. You may even be able to inspect the exact home you are interested in. You can either buy the home completed and ready to go or in its design stage, but you will only be able to take possession of the house once a sizeable portion of the development is completed. Either way, all the decisions are made for you. You are dealing with fixed prices, so there is no risk of budget overruns.

Buying 'off the plan'

As the name implies, buying off the plan means you choose a property from plans supplied by a developer. Often, each design will be linked with a block of land. Alternatively, you'll buy a unit or townhouse in a complex. The common strand here is that you are committing to something that as yet does not exist.

Incentives are common in off-the-plan packages. For example, furniture included, rent guarantees, low-rate mortgage deals. These perks are great, but calculate the *real* value of that incentive to ensure the developers are not just adding the costs of those things to the sale figure.

Timing is vital if you want to make the most of buying off the plan, because you will be more susceptible than most to market conditions. The secret here is to buy when the time is right, when the market is low in its cycle and the developers are keen to do deals.

Pros and cons of buying off the plan

There are pros and cons of buying off the plan.

Pros of buying off the plan:

▲ You could be buying at a competitive price if you get in early in the development.

▲ If the market rises during the time it takes the developer to construct the dwelling, you could make a substantial profit without doing anything at all if you choose to sell it on. This is because when operating in a rising market, the developer will increase the prices on the other homes at each stage of development.

▲ An off-the-plan purchase will allow you a certain amount of choice on fittings, colour choices and specifications.

▲ A purchase of this type allows you time to decide what you want to utilise the purchase for. Will you sell it on, live in it or rent it out? You will also have time to get your finances in place before committing.

Cons of buying off the plan:

▲ You could get carried away with the developer's skilful marketing of a 'dream' and pay too much for the purchase.

▲ If the market drops during the time it takes to construct the dwelling, and other homes within the development start to have price decreases, you could find yourself with an instant loss.

▲ The scheme could take too long to be completed, or sections could remain undeveloped around your completed home.

So basically, if your plan is to make a quick buck, be aware that the market will only produce favourable conditions a couple of times each decade, and buying on the assumption that you'll get an instant profit is a very high risk tactic. If, however, you plan to live in the off-the-plan dwelling for a long time, and instant profit is not so important, then definitely consider it as an option if it really offers value for money.

Buying a new build is all about convenience. You will have the wonderful feeling of residing in what is effectively the microwave meal of the housing industry. The beauty of buying this type of home is that it's so easy. There is very little effort required when the developer has not only chosen the design but also selected the tiles, floors and fittings. The developers invariably employ professionals to make sure the house will have mass appeal.

Generally, a brand-new home will cost just a little more than its established counterpart — unless that comparable home is recently renovated to 'new home' standards or is a character/period home where that age and style sells for a premium.

When considering where to buy, think how the surrounds might change in the first year or two of living in your new home. Will there be building sites all around you? Stand on your new land and look: that open feel and that view may not still be there once everything else is built.

Warning: know what you're getting into

If you are buying without inspecting the exact property you're purchasing, it's important that you ensure you really are getting what is being proposed. I had a client who selected a unit off the plan, and chose a certain floor because the model and plans showed a window in a key position that would allow the unit to be one of a few that would have a distant river view. In this locality and market, the view would have an impact on value.

Two years later the unit was constructed without the window. Being a unit complex, inspections were not permitted by the developer's contractors until near completion. Once it was completed, the inspection took place and my client found that no window existed. Although we shouted very loudly at the developers and my client's lawyer wrote to the company's legal representatives, the developers didn't care. They had sufficient resources to battle any case my client could attempt to bring, and ended up claiming that the council would not allow the window to be built. Their attitude was clear: 'so sue us'. My client never did, because the costs were high and the chances of winning were remote.

The lesson, as always, is buyer beware!

When to buy

If you are buying a home from a housing development, try purchasing at the very start of the development before the sales office opens. Usually, developers are keen to get some early sales and they may do a deal. Alternatively, wait until the development has finished, and the developer is keen to finish up the project and move onto the next site—again, deals can be made. If you are after certain blocks in an estate and are on a waiting list, do not expect a deal.

Building your own home

If you really want a brand-new home but don't want to buy a home that someone else has built, the alternative is to buy a block of land and build the home yourself. This is a popular method of acquiring housing in Australia—you search for and secure a block of land, then either choose an off-the-plan house design or employ an architect or builder to design your dream home.

Where do I start?

In my time selling real estate in Australia, I have been shocked to discover how many people actually find a house design before buying a block of land. How can I make my feelings on this practice clear? How about: 'You are bloody mad!'

Yes, I know it is tempting: you know you want to build a new home, so you start looking at display homes. You fall in love with a home, and then look at all blocks on the basis that they might fit your Princess Cleopatra Version 3.56 house. But you just can't do this! You will end up with so many compromises. For example, if the display home you choose is on a corner block, and the block that you chose was not on a corner block, the extra windows to one side that made the home feel so bright will not feature in your scenario.

The reason you must start with land is the same reason all property searches must start with price: if you do not know how much your land will be, how do you know how much you can spend on the house itself? Similarly, the location of your block of land will have a huge impact on the overall experience of your new house: even your dream home will not be a dream for long if you can't afford to live anywhere near your desired location, and now the school you've chosen for your kids is an hour's drive away.

A bit of an exaggeration maybe, but it is a vital consideration. If you are planning to buy land and build, secure your block first. Most project builders ask if you have your land ready—if you do, you will discover that they are very keen to help, and they may be a little bit more flexible on prices and terms as they'll see you as an immediate sale possibility, not just a dreamer.

How much should I spend?

Your budget will dictate everything from the location of your block to its size and specifications, so get that sorted first. For more on budgets, see chapter 1.

Generally, you should expect to spend more on building the house than on the purchase of the land. If you spend too little on the build in relation to the land value, you run the risk of undercapitalising on the 'package'—you could find that your home looks decidedly ordinary for its street or suburb. But be careful: if you spend too much on the build in relation to the land purchase price, you could find that you have a home too good for its location.

If you have a target value of $500 000 (this price should reflect the amount you think the house will be worth when it's completed) you should pay between $200 000 and $225 000 for the land. The costs of building the house should be the balance—between $275 000 and $300 000.

Building your McMansion

When it comes to building a new home, people often make huge errors when it comes to judging the future target market. This can make their home very difficult to sell in the future. Alternatively, many people get carried away with huge overspending after the building of the home commences. A classic error that I personally find hilarious is the nice tidy estate street with nice, solid, standard homes. Then, in the middle, is a bloody great mansion — you know, the type with more pillars than the Colosseum, a three-car garage that only just fits on the block, high walls and very obvious security (because the owners know that their extravagant McMansion is like a beacon to the local criminal element).

Okay so this is a bit of an exaggeration, but a home that's too big or too grand for its location will probably be hard to sell, so unless you want to live in your idiosyncratic home forever, you need to try to match your home's specifications to the area. By way of explanation, imagine the following scenario: median house prices in a suburb are at $538 000. The people who have bought a block and built the McMansion have spared no expense, so the McMansion has to be sold for $800 000 just to cover its costs. Most buyers in that area do not want to spend that much money, and those that *can* afford to spend that much are looking in the more expensive areas. So the McMansion either remains unsold, or it sells at a huge loss.

A good balance to aim for is to spend 40 to 45 per cent of your funds on the land, and 55 to 60 per cent on the building. So, if you anticipate living in the home long term and you find the perfect block for you at a slightly higher percentage of your available funds, a small overspend may be acceptable—but you do need to be aware of it: if not carried out carefully, the overspend can have significant consequences, including huge losses when it comes to re-selling your home, or an unacceptable compromise to your lifestyle.

Buying land is an exercise in vision, imagination, research and thinking ahead.

How do I choose the right suburb?

There is a huge variety of factors that will influence your choice of suburb, the most important of which is your budget. But even having set a budget, there are many things to consider when choosing where to buy land to build your new home: do you want to live closer to the city in an established suburb, or further out in a new estate?

Established suburbs

Established suburbs will obviously have limited land for sale, and this lack of availability may dictate your selection. Also, if availability is very limited, prices could be too high—and this may be a sign to look elsewhere. If the only blocks for sale are poorly placed or the wrong size, remember that no matter how good the home you build is, if the block is wrong you will struggle to sell in the future.

The advantage of an established suburb is that you know up front what the street and your neighbours' homes look like, and how much privacy you will have. Filling your block with the home is a much more recent trend. You can expect a similar style and aesthetic to continue in the established suburb for the fore-seeable future, because the local council dictates some of the specifications that must be adhered to when building new homes.

Because the character of the street is already established, it is important to create a home that blends in with other homes in the area (see the box on McMansions on page 79 for further discussion). So avoid established locations that may not be 'right' for your planned home, but embrace them if the environment suits what you want to create.

Housing developments

Buying blocks of land on housing developments is a most popular choice for new homebuilders.

Housing developments have changed a lot in the last few decades. In the past, housing developments comprised a few blocks of land and some simple infrastructure and basic services. You could build whatever kind of home you wanted, house your caravan in your front yard and let your pit bull run wild and eat children if you so desired.

Today's housing estates are trying to improve their image, and this has been all for the good, I say. There are now features such as parks for the kids, barbeque areas, lakes, walkways and bike tracks. Some developments even have communal pools, tennis courts and full-blown recreational clubs, not to mention gates surrounding the entire development and the provision of security services. Do not forget that the more facilities provided by the development, the more chance there is that you'll have to pay for these features each month in body corporate or strata fees.

One of the positives of building in a housing development can be the detailed covenants that may be in place. Covenants are designed to create a certain standard within the estate, generally with an aim of encouraging the aesthetics of the estate. Some may feel that these restrictions are a bit 'big brother' and also a bit of a pain, as they can dictate some of the design specifications to which you must adhere. For example, in some places, the covenants can require that the development approves your designs before you build.

Common features controlled by covenants include:

- minimum or maximum size of homes built
- architectural style
- roofing materials
- finishes
- paint colours
- height of garages

- 🏠 style and material used to build fences and boundaries between homes
- 🏠 whether or not residents can park caravans and boats on their block.

The features of these covenants are available for prospective buyers to read before they purchase. It's a good idea to read these carefully before you start planning the specifications of your house.

Eco friendly developments

I came across a development that was 'eco friendly focused'. The developers of this estate encouraged keeping chooks, sheep and the odd goat, and they encouraged residents to grow their own veggies — but the covenant stated that you couldn't have cats and dogs! Yes, those covenants are getting more and more creative.

I do feel that if a development has sensible and focused guidelines in their covenants, the chances are the development will age well and be a very pleasant place to live and invest in.

How do I make sure I choose the right site?

If you've successfully decided what kind of suburb you'd like to live in, the next step is to choose a site. There is much argument as to whether a sloping or flat block is the best option for building a new house, for example. I personally love sloping sites because they give you views and an opportunity to design a more creative home. But along with these benefits come increased building costs. Be careful to remember your budget here—building a home on a level block will be easier.

Things to check

There are a number of things that you should consider when choosing your block. These include:

🏠 *Soil report.* Before you build anything, you will need to enlist the services of a specialist (often a geotechnical engineer) to assess the quality of the soil on which your house is to be build. This is crucial because rocky land and sandy soil for example can increase the costs over the normal builder's allowance. Land is classified in reference to its soil type, its stability and its drainage. Standard classifications are: Class A—no worries mate; Class S—still no real worries pal; Class M—getting a little trickier; Class H—hmmm, getting really tricky now; Class E—oh dear, this could be very costly!; and Class P—give in, and go home! These classifications are a simple way to evaluate how cheap or expensive the build may be. Talk to the surveyor who inspected the land and classified it—he or she may have some pearls of wisdom.

🏠 *Drainage.* It is important to understand how water and other liquids will be drained from the site you're inspecting. You should discuss this with your architect or builder, because it is often conveniently omitted from some builders' initial quotes and costs. Councils rightly impose certain rules about the disposal of water on a block (and no, you can't just divert the water directly into your closest neighbour's land, before you get any ideas…)

🏠 *Position of the sun.* You should consider the natural movement of the sun when choosing a site. The type of home you build will be affected by this. For example, if you choose a design that features a wall of huge windows on the northern elevation of your block, you are likely to get sunburnt while watching TV in the lounge room! Similarly, you would hate to build a dwelling and find out later that you don't get any natural light inside. Get this element of the build right at the design stage and the liveability of your home will be enhanced immeasurably.

🏠 *Shape of the block.* The house you choose will be directly contingent on the shape and size of the block you choose, for obvious reasons. There are really only a few shapes of block. These include the square or rectangular block (this is the easiest to construct a home on, and most project home builders design their homes for this land parcel shape); the fan-shaped block that is very wide at the front. This style allows for a stunning frontage to be created, but the narrow back can cause problems. The other fan shape is narrow at the front and wide to the rear, facilitating the construction of gardens, pools and entertaining spaces. Finally there is the 'battle-axe block', which has very little street frontage and can be surrounded by other homes, so a design needs to be creative.

- *Access to services.* Obviously, you will need to ensure your block can be accessed easily because a simple connection to water, drainage, electricity or gas could be difficult if you buy in a remote area.

- *Potential for fire hazard.* The recent bushfires around Australia have reminded us all of the importance of considering a block's vulnerability to fire. Especially in rural areas, it's vital to ensure your home has features to assist its protection against fire. Your local fire station will always give information. Many areas actually have their risk of fire classified as low, medium or high. If your land falls into the high-risk category, don't panic—just get the right advice.

- *Potential for flood hazard.* If the home you plan to build is on or near the water, it's important to consider the risk of flood when choosing the land. Your architect or local council will be able to advise you on the area's risk of flood, and on potential building strategies that you can use to minimise the risk of damage. In the meantime, if your property is at risk of floods get yourself some good flood insurance and keep a tinny in the roof space.

- *Proximity of main roads:* Main roads can have an impact on any suburb, but modern developments seem to plan housing that backs onto main roads as common practice. The houses that back onto the main road are always hardest re-sell, so either avoid them or expect to buy them at a decent discount. A home facing a main road where the rear yard is away from the road is far less of an issue. Why councils continue to encourage this planning stupidity I do not know. Your build will cost the same, but the value of the completed home will be as much as 10 or 15 per cent less than its better-situated neighbour.

Green specifications

A new prototype home with a mind-blowing nine-star energy rating has been created by one of Australia's large developers. If that means nothing to you, remember that five stars are pretty damn good! The home is constructed on a 100 per cent recyclable concrete slab, and will feature a revolutionary reverse brick veneer structure (yes, that means the timber frame on the outside and the bricks on the inside). The house also sports incredible levels of insulation, double-glazed north-facing windows, cross ventilation, solar power electricity and hot water, rainwater tanks and an abundance of recycled materials. Price? Undisclosed! But it does demonstrate that if you plan to build soon or in the future, you should take this 'green' thing very seriously.

If you feel that checking all these things might be too much to organise on your own, the following experts can help you to do the research on the site of your choice:

- builders
- engineers
- plumbers
- electricians
- architects
- local council.

All the above professionals will be a fantastic source of information, but all will want payment except for the local council.

> **Local council**
>
> The council could actually be your best source of information when planning, because they effectively represent the state and federal governments, so the council is your one-stop shop for free information and is literally a phone call or a click of the mouse away.
>
> Councils regulate zoning, which will have all sorts of implications for your building plans. They will also have regulations that dictate what you can legally build on the land. They also have building standards for construction projects.

Design and construction

Once you have decided to build a home rather than buy a new build, successfully made a budget and purchased a piece of land you like, it's time to move on to the fun part: choosing or designing a new home that's right for you, and watching it materialise.

Match your design to your block

One of the most common mistakes made by Australian buyers is failure to ensure that the home they plan to build is compatible with the block of land they have bought. I blame builders for failing to stop their clients building horrible homes, or not advising their clients well enough. Builders build hundreds of homes that are either poorly orientated or designed incorrectly for the block. You may not think this is important, but when you come to sell your house people will notice.

A common building mistake is to rush your decision on specifications. Take your time and listen to the experts. If you select badly, expect to own a home that is very hard to sell and that will always be the ugly duckling of the street. Don't think you can hide from me—I will spot your home easily if you fail, as will other agents. In conjunction with your builder or architect, make carefully considered decisions about every element of the home, including:

- orientation of the house
- floor plan
- materials used
- internal fittings
- ceiling heights
- colour schemes
- position of power sockets
- external finishes
- roof tiles
- fencing
- length of driveway
- pathways.

To avoid costly mistakes, demand exact and detailed specifications from the builder, and make sure you are familiar with the land you are building on. Check, in particular, whether your block has building covenants to which you must adhere.

Sustainable building practices

When choosing the materials you use for building your new home, always try to minimise the environmental impact of the construction by using recycled, sustainable or composite materials. Not only is this good for the planet, but it can make you money in the long term. This is because there is an increasing level of demand for homes that are set up for green living. When it comes time to sell your home, you will almost certainly get a higher sale price if your home is sustainably built — so by using sustainable materials at the building stage, you are adding value to your home.

Sustainable building practices (cont'd)

Recycled materials are made from reused materials, and are designed to reduce wastage, landfill, carbon emissions and water consumption. These may include reclaimed bricks or blocks and composite timber-based products made from off cuts or wood waste.

Sustainable materials are new, but come from a source where the materials used in their production is easily replaced or sustainable. Many timber products are now available from plantation rather than old-growth rain forests, or from forests that are continually regenerated to compensate for the environmental impact of the materials extracted from them. For more information, visit <www.forestrystandard.org.au>.

Composite materials are items made up of a mixture of elements to produce a substitute 'look alike' product. Often, the product is made from recycled ingredients and as such has a lower environmental impact than its non-composite counterpart has.

If you decide to employ an architect to design your house, he or she will be able to advise you on what sort of specifications are realistic and what sort of specifications just won't work with your budget or the block you've chosen.

Using a project home builder

A project home builder is a building company that builds a set number of house designs in bulk, and then sells them individually. Some project home builders will allow you to make changes to the house plan, and you can often go and check out a display home to decide on the design specifications you want. Buying a project home can save you time, as you won't need to design the home yourself or hire an architect. Also, build times are generally very short, and often the companies that manage homes employ tradespeople who have built the same design several times before, which can result in fewer mistakes in the construction process.

I think many of these 'off-the-plan' houses offer a good alternative for many homebuyers. I will add a word of warning: be aware that the display home you fall in love with is usually displayed with the top-of-the-line specifications rather than the standard ones, so if your budget will only stretch to the standard fittings you might be disappointed with the end product, and it may be harder to re-sell than you originally thought.

If you do choose to go with the top specifications, expect to pay between 25 and 50 per cent more than the base price. To undertake changes in specification after the build is too late and too costly, so it's important to make your decision up front.

Working with an architect to design your own home

Unless you have links with the building industry, you should always consider the option of hiring an architect. In my experience, I've found that the only reason buyers avoid this option is because of the perceived costs. Don't dismiss this option until you have contacted a few architects and obtained quotes to see if they can meet your target budget. It is a good idea to ask the architect to act as manager for the construction process—their invaluable expertise will ensure your home becomes something special.

Often, an architect-designed home is more flexible, but a project home can be more efficient to build (although it may not be the only one in the suburb!). With the latter option, you see a design, make a few changes (good ones I hope) and off you go. With the former, you and the architect will start with a dream, which is usually drastically altered after you discuss your budget, so be prepared to be flexible throughout the design process, and adjust your expectations as required.

That said, good architects know wonderful ways of cutting costs in design and with materials and finishes, with little impact on the outcome of the home. Good style is not necessarily about big budgets. I should know—I live on the Gold Coast! I constantly witness examples of huge-budget homes with about as much style, flair and ambiance as a trailer park.

So do consider the architect-designed option, but expect to be more involved in the project and be ready to work with the architect as a team.

Here are some things to keep in mind when working with an architect who is designing your home:

- *Decide on your budget.* This will depend on your personal finances, but do not disclose your final budget at the initial meeting. Architects will tend to work to this figure, giving you very little room to manoeuvre for the inevitable overspends. Try suggesting 10 to 15 per cent *less* than you really have available to build in the probability of overspends.

- *List your must-haves.* Ensure the architect knows exactly what you're after. If possible, do some sketches and take pictures of homes you like, or take magazines so the architect can really get a feel for what you want.

- *Look at the architect's previously completed projects.* This will help you decide whether you like his or her style of design, and whether you are happy with the materials used.

- *Be open minded.* Consider fresh ideas and suggestions and new or alternative materials. Architects are a great source of information, and their flair for ideas is one of the elements you are paying for.

- *Check on guarantees and warranties.* Ensure that you're familiar with the terms of the guarantees and warranties offered. Get your lawyer to look over contracts, and ask him or her what happens if the builder goes into receivership during construction.

- *Establish the viability of matching your budget to your desired specification.* Tell the architect the ideal size and specifications of your home. Be sure to include as many things as possible from the list on page 87. This will give the architect an idea as to whether your budget is feasible. If it's not, you'll have to compromise.

🏠 *Match your design to your land.* As mentioned earlier in the chapter, it's vital to ensure your design is a good match with your chosen block.

Make sure you get what you want

Whichever route you take to build your brand-new house, whether you employ a project home builder or an architect, make sure you get what you want. It can be worth involving your lawyer; the agreement with the builder to construct your home is a contract, and a very pricey one, too, so its details need to be right for you.

When you are meeting with builders or architects, always stand your ground—in many cases, these professionals see you as just another client, and they may need to be reminded that the project they're working on is your home.

 Don't get bullied into making design choices that may not suit you, your lifestyle or your personality.

Standing your ground doesn't mean you should ignore valid advice. Architects and builders will have suggestions and ideas that can make your new home that extra little bit special, and they can certainly advise you when it comes to making hard decisions.

Here are some tips that will make sure you always get what you want from architects and builders:

🏠 Never be afraid to ask questions.

🏠 Establish what the costs will be for any extras or changes—if the costs are high, ask why and whether there's an alternative.

🏠 If you're not happy with any of their suggestions, look up alternatives online and suggest politely that they look into your research.

- Avoid conflict where possible.

- Involve your lawyer in important or costly decisions.

- Consider specialised insurance to protect you against the developer going bust during construction—they usually like to do this after you have made another stage payment.

The most successful projects happen when you work closely with the architect and the builder. Aim to diffuse tension and avoid bitter disputes—if you don't, you may find that the builders 'accidentally' fail to connect the sewage waste pipes.

So should you buy or build new? Only you can decide. Because of the huge number of options for new home buyers I would categorically state you should never avoid this option—it may suit your requirements at some point of your buying career.

Buying a new home can be a great purchase at certain points in the property market cycle, but disastrous at other times. Never let your guard slip—research is just as important for a new home-buyer as it is for someone looking to buy an established home.

. . . .

What's the agent thinking?

Okay, I know most new homes are not sold directly by trad-itional real estate agents—but some are. The developers that often sell new builds are just as intelligent and sales orientated as agents are, and they know what gets the buying public excited. Unlike traditional real estate agents and sellers of established homes, developers can design a product to meet the local market. When constructing display homes, a good developer will research the typical buyer—*you*. So here are some of their tricks exposed.

Offers of deposit paid, legal fees included, stamp duty free and cash back are popular sales tactics. Don't be fooled: all they are doing is adding the so-called 'free' element on to the price of the product you're buying.

Another common incentive used to lure unsuspecting buyers in is the promise of 'buy now and settle in two years'. This can be good in a rising market: you secure at today's value. But it is very good for developers, too, because they haven't built anything yet but still have your financial commitment to buy, so only buy like this if you are getting a great deal.

Developers may offer to pay your mortgage for a certain period or guarantee your rental income. These offers can be very tempting, but ask yourself: what is the value to you? Establish what you think the home is worth, and if the home's value plus one year's mortgage payment is the same, you know where you stand. Often, the purchase price minus one year's mortgage repayment is still more than the home's true value — so watch out!

Trading up

Chapter 5

Moving to a home with more

Trading up is when the fun starts in most people's home-buying careers. Trading up happens when you have worked hard for years, and can finally afford to spend real money on a mortgage. You therefore have more equity, and can afford to move into a bigger, better-located and more beautiful home. In other words, you are ready to move up the proverbial property ladder.

Andrew's hot tip

Equity refers to the amount by which the market value of your property exceeds your level of debt. It is calculated by working out the market value of the home, and subtracting the amount still owing in mortgage repayments. At the time of purchase, the equity is the same in monetary terms as the deposit, unless the market value suddenly moves up or down. Equity is built over a period of time, and is based on how a property's value increases or decreases.

95

The life cycle of a homeowner's buying plan

Prior to analysing all the facts about trading up, I want to explain how I see the life cycle of the average homeowner's buying plan. I refer to a 'plan' because most people do have a rough plan when they start out, and indeed a good long-term plan can ensure you avoid a wasted, costly and pointless move.

Australian averages for the length of time of owning a single home differ between generations and locations. On average, though, Aussies move every five to seven years. On that basis, if an average first homeowner is in their late 20s and he or she continues to move until their mid 70s, we can conclude that Australians tend to move houses between seven and 10 times in their lifetime. For the purposes of this chapter, I am only referring to the principal residence—many of us find ourselves in rentals for the short term to fill gaps, or when moving to new areas.

Genuine trade ups only really happen a few moves into your purchasing career. Following is a typical home-buying pattern based on what I have seen in the Australian property market.

First home

Your first home will often be a small unit or townhouse— usually in a slick, urban inner-city area. Young people buy here so they can go out and have fun and then be able to walk home afterwards, because they may have had to sell the car to afford this first pad. It is a good idea to retain your first home for as long as you can to build up equity.

Second home

Your second home could be a townhouse or small freestanding house in a quiet suburb a bit further out from the CBD than your first home. This may seem like a 'sideways' move because the actual home you move in to may not differ much from the previous one, but it may have some small improvements such as more interior space or a slightly better location. By moving out a bit further, you'll get a bit more space—maybe space for child number one, or for mates to stay and help out with the mortgage.

Third home

By the time you buy your third house, you may be able to afford a decent-sized freestanding home that gives you enough space for a second child and enough room to grow. By now, you will have different location requirements: distance to schools and parks will become more important than distance to nightclubs and the CBD.

Fourth home

Home number four can be one of the most important moves most people will make: it's the big family home with the space you need for your partner and kids. By 'big' I'm also referring to the size of the cost of buying and maintaining the property, and the associated costs that go along with it (such as stamp duty and agent fees). To avoid wasting time, money and effort, you really need to get this one right. You'll probably move into a home you would never have dreamed of living in back when you bought your first home. Hopefully by now you will have a fair amount of equity built up. Your choice of suburb here is vital—schools for the kids, work places and other amenities all need to be handy. The issue of long-term capital growth needs to be considered, too, because you will probably plan to stay here long term.

This seems to be the point in the life cycle where people either find themselves ticking along nicely or getting blown out of the water by major work or business issues, personal disasters or random occurrences that have a negative impact on their comfortable lives. Disasters hit everyone at some point—the nicest people, and the ones we don't care about such as tax auditors. Divorce or separation can necessitate moves that are almost never trading up, as the scramble to find a home quickly and cheaply usually takes priority over creature comforts or long-term investment plans.

Andrew's hot tip

Many people incorrectly assume that they will spend their lives moving *up* the property ladder. However, if you're like most homeowners, you almost invariably climb down again at some point. This traditionally occurs at the end of your purchasing life cycle, but climb-downs can occur at unexpected and unplanned intervals, so be prepared to be flexible.

The lucky ones remain in their fourth home because they love it and only move when age or ill health dictates a downsize. Some continue to maintain and increase their income, in which case they may be able to trade up again. The unlucky ones decide that enough is enough and split up and sell the home. Others find that their income is not sustainable, and down the ladder they go.

Fifth home

The purchase of the fifth home is another potentially defining move. You'll either be headed up, up and away to another grand home, or down, down, down because life has progressed along a rather unexpected route. For the purposes of this chapter, let's imagine that all is going well. This move is likely to be the big one — the largest in value of all the homes you buy. You will probably remain in this home for many years, and the home's value will increase along with your equity. This will result in a large amount of cash, which will allow you to fund future moves or an extremely comfortable retirement.

Alternatively, move five can be a sideways move in to a home of a similar value to house number four, but different in form — for example, a smaller home in a more exclusive suburb. If you plan to make a sideways move, ensure you analyse it carefully and can see the benefits. Keep in mind that even if you sell your current $700 000 home and purchase a new $700 000 home, you will be up for extra costs in removals and new furniture if you go down a different decorating path plus the usual moving expenses.

Homes six through 10

The number of moves you embark on after home number four or five depends on you. If you smoke 50 cigarettes a day, your exercise is limited to standing at the bar, the barbie and the occasional standing ovation for your footy team and you consume enough alcohol and pure fat to make even the move to your fifth home a pleasant surprise, then you're unlikely to have to worry about further moves.

Those of you who intend to live to a ripe old age will probably consider selling your big home and trading down. Unfortunately, the final moves in your housing career often involve living in a converted double garage next to one of your kids. (Your kids, of course, will demand a substantial sum of your now-diminishing equity for this privilege.) Alternatively, you may decide to hand your money over to some lovely resident manager at The Palms Resort Homes for the More Mature. Here, you'll spend your days playing bridge and lawn bowls in a state-of-the-art facility that has no stairs, plenty of handrails, 24-hour medical staff and wipe-clean floors: perfect! As you can see, without trading up in your youth, you'd never be able to afford this level of comfort in your twilight years. I suppose that if you had no money, the government would have to pay for your retirement accommodation. Hmmm. Oh well, I am sure there is *some* reason to trade up!

Why trade up?

The sole purpose of trading up is to provide you with a home that has *more*. 'More' can be defined in a number of ways, including:

- more space
- a better location
- better features: style, view or design
- more money to be earned
- higher social status.

Yes, you may actually need some of these 'mores', but remember that the home-buying plan I outlined earlier only works if you financially stretch yourself. So work out which 'mores' you are willing to sacrifice for, but don't be shallow or indiscriminate about your decisions—you will end up losing time and money for no real gain (see the section 'the wasted move' later in this chapter). To make the most of your trade up, you need to sensibly define what you really want. Ask yourself the following questions:

- Is your existing home really so bad?

- Do you really *need* to trade up?

- Why do you need more?

- Will a trade up really improve your lifestyle?

- Will a trade up financially benefit you?

- Is the precise location of your current home a real winner with your lifestyle?

- Could you gain all you need by adding a bedroom or an extra bathroom, or by updating the fittings? Improvements can add value, so this could be a sensible option.

If you've considered all these questions and you are still sure that trading up is going to benefit you in the long term, there are a few things to consider; for example: where should you buy? What kind of house should you buy? What are the financial implications of moving? And is a perceived increase in social status a good enough reason to trade up?

Location

'Trading up' should be a move to a more desirable (and expensive) location. Quite often, a suburb will have a variety of differently valued areas within it, so trading up can literally involve moving to the other side of the road, or up the hill.

When trading up, you must ensure the area you are buying in really is a true 'step up'; just because your sister lives there does not make it 'better'. A 'better' location will often be characterised by higher average house prices than your suburb, and a noticeable improvement to your quality of house.

Different house types

Moving to a different type of house could mean moving to a bigger house, or deciding to trade up to a historic or character-filled period home. It could also mean a move to a contemporary home from an older-style home, or trading up from a traditionally laid-out residence to an open-plan entertainer. The most common thing people look for when they upgrade to a different type of house is more space. There are no hard-and-fast rules about what to look for when trading up, but here are some common ones:

- moving to a quieter street

- getting a larger block if living in family orientated areas

- getting a second parking spot in urban areas.

Financial benefit

Put in simple terms, the financial reason to trade up is this: if done properly, a trade up should result in a value increase over a few years that is greater than the increase you would get on your existing home. As this money is tied up in your property, you can't spend it, so when it comes time to sell, you will achieve a healthy profit that will increase your overall wealth substantially.

The main exception to this rule is when buying investment properties for the purpose of renting them to tenants. This is because the monthly rental income attained for expensive homes is much lower than the monthly mortgage repayments on such houses. At the lower end of the market, the rental income should come close to covering the mortgage repayments. This is because generally, renters are reluctant to spend extravagant amounts of money on renting. If they could afford to do that, they'd just buy. For example, a $400 000 home could attract a rental income of $400 per week, which may cover the owner's repayments on a 90 per cent loan. An $800 000 home may get only $700 per week, and as such will not cover the mortgage repayments plus running costs on the bigger home.

Social status

Of course, status is a huge motivator when trading up: you want a bigger home, a better location, a cooler style of home—all because your mates will think: 'Wow'. Don't knock it, because shallowness keeps our modern residential market ticking over. Of course, I have never personally succumbed to a shallow approach when considering trading up. (If you believe that, you'll also believe that I am Brad Pitt's twin brother.)

Now I know we live in Australia, and some people think we don't have a class system here, but as an agent, I often witness the power that social status has when property decisions are being made. For example, that woman over there claiming that she needs extra space for her growing family? She already has a four-bed, two-bath home with a double garage. But so do her mates. Her family's income, if pushed, will allow the purchase of a five-bed, four-bath, three-car-garage home. It will only be a few hundred metres from their existing home, but it will be *so* much better than her friends' places!

One agent only recently told me a story that confirms all my feelings about the subject of status in the Australian real estate market. He had been working with a very lucky family who had done very well for themselves and were living in what can only be described as a waterfront mansion with a healthy price tag of $3 000 000. Despite its huge price tag and stunning water aspect, the block was only about 850 square metres in size.

After running into recent financial difficulty, the family was in a panic. Things had been tough, and they needed to downsize.

Oh my God! *Downsize* at *their* age and stage of life? Socially, it was totally impossible for them to consider moving to a nearby suburb into a modest—and, to them, embarrassing—$2 000 000 home, even though the new home would give them all the features they would need in terms of aspect, location and features, and would, for most of us, also ooze the requisite 'snob value'. The family simply did not want to be seen as downsizing.

So they announced to all of their friends and family that they were trading up to a larger property because they wanted a lifestyle change—of course failing to mention the fact that they would be clearing a million dollars off their rather massive debt.

So how did they achieve this very clever and cunning move? They moved to nearby acreage in a cheaper suburb and into a home that was equally big, but that also had stunning and extensive gardens, a tennis court, big gates—the lot! When presented with a home such as this one, no-one would really know what the price tag was, nor should they care, because these clever folk had described their decision as a 'lifestyle change'. I love this story because it epitomises the real reasons for a trade up, and that is the fact that people just want 'more.'

Andrew's hot tip What would you be leaving behind if you were to trade up? Do your homework really well. If it is dreadful neighbours, too little space, a floor plan that just doesn't work anymore for your family's needs or you are just bored with the home — that is all okay, but you really need to be honest with yourself.

How much should you spend to see a benefit?

If you can only afford to trade up by 15 per cent or less of your existing home's value, it is hardly worth calling it a trade up. Ideally, you should be aiming to spend 20 per cent more than the value of your house.

For example, if you own a $400 000 home and buy another home in the same suburb for $440 000 (an additional 10 per cent of your home's value), you are unlikely to see much of a benefit in terms of lifestyle changes. However, if you spend $480 000 in the same suburb (an additional 20 per cent of your home's value), you really should start to see an improvement. Further, moving house is expensive; you need to pay for a whole host of expenses such as stamp duty, removal costs, agent fees, advertising fees and the potential cost of redecorating your new place. Because of these added expenses, you might not make much financial progress at all if you spend all that money to move into a new house that is not much more valuable than your existing one.

 A successful trade up

A colleague of mine (he claims to be TV's best cameraman) recently traded up, after years of nagging by his lovely wife.

After analysing their finances and considering the costs of the trade up, they decided a trade up of a certain value would improve their lifestyle and give them a good long-term investment, too. So they put their home on the market, sold it, secured a new home and off they went!

This trade up equated to about 25 to 30 per cent, and the best part is they knew, and others could clearly see, the trade up was worthwhile. The suburb was a little better (but only a little), the new street featured bigger blocks and more expensive homes, and (perhaps most importantly) their new home was newer, about 30 per cent larger and on a bigger block than their previous place.

The trade up really improved the family's lifestyle — in fact, my colleague now claims his new master suite is so big he is considering subdivision!

This type of situation is an example of where a trade up is a very worthwhile endeavour.

The wasted move

No, I'm not referring to a move undertaken while under the influence. I'm talking about a poorly thought-out move that fails to benefit your lifestyle enough to warrant the expense. A trade up should, in the long run, make you money and improve your lifestyle. If you have moved for the wrong reasons and therefore chosen poorly, you could be facing a very costly error.

Social climbers beware: people often trade up locations but cannot afford a decent-sized home in their new locale. So despite spending more money and having the benefit of a prestigious address, the home will result in an unhappy family and the certainty of another move — often at a financial loss.

In stark contrast, the move to a big, grand home in a less appealing or less convenient suburb is another common trade up error. Yes, you love the new home, but if the location is second-rate compared with your previous home you will still find your lifestyle compromised, and that will mean agents in and a 'for sale' board up before you can say 'negative equity'!

Like all decisions you make in property, it's really important to find a sensible compromise. Losing space so you can afford to move to a posh suburb or gaining space at the expense of convenience and friendly neighbours are just not sensible solutions.

Keeping your head

It's really important to keep your wits about you and really think about the perils and positives of trading up before taking the plunge. I'd like to share a possible future scenario with you that will illustrate how easy it can be to get caught up in the excitement of trading up without actually considering the consequences.

Imagine that one night over a takeaway Thai dinner while watching *Dancing with the Stars* and *Selling Houses Australia,* you and your partner discuss the prospect of moving up the property ladder. You want somewhere a bit bigger, and on the 'right' side of town. You know what type of house you want because you've looked on the internet, and everyone loves your place so selling it won't be a problem. Your in-depth conversation has not included financial analysis or meetings with advisers or banks, and it certainly hasn't included a visit from local agents to assess your home for market.

You decide on Saturday morning after the kids have gone out for their weekend activities that you should check out some open for inspections—no preparation, no financial advice and no real idea about anything. You are like lambs to the slaughter—an agent's ideal client!

Off to inspections you go. The first four houses fail to impress you. In fact, you feel very self-satisfied because your home is loads better than the ones you've looked at. You think the sellers have no taste and the agents are dreaming.

But on inspection number five, things pan out quite differently. You arrive at the address, and park your car out the front of the house. The very sight of the house makes you go instantly quiet. You and your partner look around at the street environment; then you look back to one another, eyes wide and smiles spreading across your faces. This home is a *dream*! You walk in through the front door, still dumbstruck, where you are greeted by the agent. Within seconds the agent, who has immediately noted your obvious enthusiasm, whisks you away on a tour of this magnificent abode. As the agent has suggested, you are 'imaging yourself living in this amazing home'. (Note: the phrase 'imagine yourself living here' is commonly used on TV property shows, but here's a secret: *when those buyers say it, they never mean it*. It's when it *isn't* said that it really is being thought.) The inspection is carried out in near silence because you and your partner are so in love with the house that you can't focus on anything else. Before you know it, you are back in the car. You don't know what's hit you and, moreover, you have no idea what your parting comments to the agent were. Your silence is broken only by the mad torrent of gushing adoration and adulation about the house—in your mind, you are already packing and moving.

By the time you get home, a decision has been made: you have fallen head over heels. You start criticising your old place for no reason other than the fact that you want to convince yourself that you *need* this unexpectedly urgent move.

Now, I would normally be the first to encourage this enthusiasm. I love people that love houses, and who get a real buzz when they see the home of their dreams. It's falling in love with a house *before* you do any prep work that is the problem. But disaster *can* be avoided by not doing anything other than online research and a few drive-bys until you've done your research, checked your finances and are really and truly ready to buy.

Buy before you sell

Buying a new house without selling your existing one is fine if you can afford two homes at once, and you have prepared a backup plan to cover situations such as the existing home failing to sell quickly, or offers not being as high as expected.

If finance will not allow a purchase before selling, stop inspecting! Do not let yourself fall over at this stage—it is all about control. Trading up should be an exciting process, not an exercise in stupidity. My advice for homeowners who can't afford two houses at once, or simply want to avoid unnecessary stress, is very clear: buying a new house before you sell your old one is madness.

Plan before you inspect, or your househunting will be akin to shopping without any money.

Typical pitfalls

Trading up should carry a health warning: it has the potential to cause tension, pressure and unnecessary cardiac strain if not carried out thoughtfully and for the right reasons. There are a few key things to look out for when trading up:

▲ Avoid buying your new home before selling your existing one.

▲ Things may have changed since you last sold and bought, so make sure you're familiar with current market conditions for your area.

▲ Never expect an easy sell.

▲ Research the market and work out what your current home really has to offer. Consider upgrading your existing home to maximise its value.

▲ Almost all trading-up cases require a bigger mortgage, so be prepared and think how it will impact on your monthly budget.

Another thing to consider is making sure that you have the resources to enable a trade up of sufficient difference. Aim to spend at least 20 per cent more than you get for your current house. The reason is moving and trading up has considerable expenses that cannot be avoided, stamp duty being the biggest. Stamp duty can cost between around 3 per cent to more than 5 per cent of the value of your home, depending on your state. Because of these associated costs, unless you aim to move up 20 per cent you may not see any real lifestyle or potential financial benefits (even as your home's value grows) if you have put yourself into a financially insecure position. A sensible reason people trade up is the percentage growth of a more expensive home can help with your super plans for those later years. But only trade up if you have the financial means to do so and your thorough research is completed before you start looking. Most importantly — and a tip I always give people if you plan to trade up — ensure your new home feels like a trade up. It's hard to define but you will know, and so will your friends, if it feels like a trade up — you are doing well!

If you do fall in love with a new home prior to sorting things out you could expose yourself to a number of problems, including:

- putting yourself under immense financial pressure if you do secure the home

- ending up in a forced sale situation (see pages 144 to 147 for a discussion on forced sales), which could mean getting less than top dollar for your home (buyers love desperate sellers)

- losing out financially as you sell for less because the pressure of paying for your new home made you unable to negotiate hard for the purchase home.

Covering costs by leasing your old house

Renting out your old house to cover the expenses of the new one can sometimes be a great backup plan if you buy a second house before selling the first. But this method can sometimes be fraught with problems, so you must prepare yourself.

Landlords created by scenarios such as this are a nightmare. Because tenants are now living in your former home and because you want to sell it in the near future, you become protective over it. You expect tenants to pay more than market value often because you have decided on an unrealistic rental value, usually based on what you need to cover two mortgages. Also you are annoyed if they fail to keep the home looking like a display home at all times because you want the house to look immaculate for prospective buyers. If the tenants have more than one child under five, if they have a dog or if they want the occasional cigarette—well, you become a very demanding and tense landlord. In many cases, you would be best described as pain in the arse, as the pressure seems to ensure normally sensible people go a little mad. Here are a few reasons why:

- You could be either a first-time landlord or a landlord for your very recent home. It's only natural to be more protective than usual.

⌂ Tenants are never going to be as careful about perfect presentation or accommodating with inspections as you would be. Why would they? Inspections from potential buyers can be an intrusion into their home. Yes, it is your home you would like to sell, but they are paying you rent to live there.

⌂ There are still more pressures involved: how long do you rent out the home for? (A long tenancy could put off would-be owner-occupier buyers but short-term tenants are harder to secure, too.)

In my experience, if you do find yourself in this situation, take a long-term view to allow time to evaluate the situation. As long as rental income can contribute sufficiently in that period, it does buy you time. A year later the market may be a different place and you will not feel so panicked.

The hidden costs of buying before you sell

If you are to go down the 'buy before you sell' route, make sure you familiarise yourself with *all* the costs. Remember, these costs will be even harder to meet because if you have bought before you've sold, you will not have the sale proceeds to cover these costs. These costs include:

⌂ You'll face higher monthly repayments because you'll be stung for the second mortgage and the finance needed to buy the home without selling. So how long can you afford to pay the extra interest?

⌂ Council rates will need to be paid for both houses, which could place an unexpected strain on your finances.

⌂ Insurance—you'll now be paying for two homes, not one.

⌂ Legal costs are usually settled from the proceeds of a sale. If you have not sold yet, you'll need the cash flow to pay the legal bills.

⌂ Stamp duty, like the legals, is usually covered by the sale of the property. Think carefully as this large sum has to be funded somehow. It can often add up to nearly as much as six to 12 months of extra mortgage payments.

🏠 The need to spend considerable sums on your old home to attract tenants or buyers, or to comply with your local council's statutory regulations, could mean unexpected spending that you hadn't budgeted for.

Trading up is, I believe, one of the best ways to make money for the future. It allows you to get a great home while building equity, as well as the freedom to trade down when you're ready and have another decent home, mortgage free.

Do not rush into your move, as tempting as this may be. Instead, take your time to get your old house back on the market, and assess the next level of housing. Don't inspect new houses until your finances are ready or you have sold your existing home. This way you avoid an awful lot of stress, and you may actually have some hair left at the end of the process.

If you do it right, your new home will have that elusive 'more' you were looking for at the beginning.

. . . .

What's the agent thinking?

Agents love people in the market to trade up. You are potentially the double deal—in an agent's ideal world, you see a home, fall in love, commit to it, then realise you have to sell your present home. So the agent gets a sale *and* a new listing with automatically motivated sellers! If the banks are mad enough to let you buy your new house before you sell your old one, your existing home becomes a forced sale—and you won't be negotiating from a position of strength, so the agent knows a deal will be done.

If you so happen to inspect a home and fall in love, *please* don't let the agent, or seller, know about your reaction until you have decided how you can proceed. This is the most common house-buying mistake I see.

Watch out for the 'pressure sell'. Claims may be made that numerous other buyers are interested, but ignore the agent. This is the oldest trick in the book. To be fair it can be true in some cases, but this is irrelevant if you are not in a position to buy. A good agent will give you time.

Note the agent's sales techniques: the cheeky ones will push, where the professional ones will understand your situation and work with it. Go with the professional ones.

Buying to make money

Chapter 6

The wild world of property investment

So, you want to make money from real estate, eh?

It should be easy, shouldn't it? There's so much information out there! Statistics are available at the click of a mouse; there are impressive, flashy information seminars and conferences to attend; property experts are everywhere; TV shows will show you how easy it all is; investment specialists will guarantee high levels of rental income; magazines list innumerable success stories and there are books—so many books! In just a short afternoon of research, you could be bombarded with any of the following questions:

🏠 What should I be buying? A unit or a house? A fixer-upper or freshly renovated? A new house in a new development or a new shoebox in the inner city? A commercial investment or a residential investment property?

🏠 Which suburb should I target?

⌂ How should I finance my purchase?

⌂ How should I make it tax efficient?

⌂ How much money can I make?

⌂ When can I retire to my mansion—mortgage free? (This wildly ambitious claim isn't as crazy as it seems—or that is what some of the more questionable 'investment specialists' would have you think. If it sounds too good to be true, it probably is.)

So how do you plough through the information overload and discover the truth about investing in property? Well, that question is actually easy to answer: you listen to me, because I know what I'm talking about and can assure you that most of the information out there is rubbish. As you'll see, the questions you should actually be asking yourself before you invest in property are completely different to the questions that are usually answered in the media or at sensationalist property seminars. But more on that later in the chapter.

Property investment has become a popular endeavour since the '90s because of the availability of finance. For perhaps the first time in history, ordinary people have been able to finance more than one property at a time, whereas in previous generations, all the average person could generally afford was to trade up after selling their family home. Buying second or third homes for no other reason than to make money was simply not possible. Back in the '70s and '80s, the lucky people who had a second property either had a hobby farm, a holiday home or a property owned by the family for generations that they had inherited—and these types of houses certainly weren't considered to be investment vehicles for the average punter!

So what is an investment property, really? 'Property investment' is a term used by many savvy real estate agents and corporate developers to attract buyers seeking to make money from property. The odd thing about this term is that, short of really bad luck, *every* residential property will make its owner some money eventually. So in reality, *every* residential property is an investment property. But, for the purposes of this book, when I say 'investment property' I am referring to a property that the buyer plans to utilise as an *additional* property to their residential one, and that has been purchased for the sole purpose of making money.

I have personally had some great experiences with investment properties. Contrary to popular belief, real estate is not the best-paid industry in the world; most of my money has been made by investing in housing over the years. Because of this, I genuinely believe that property is an excellent investment vehicle. The reason for this is that, unlike stocks or shares, housing is a tangible asset that can be seen, touched and usually controlled by you personally.

The majority of people who enter the world of property investment will do absolutely fine. Of course, they may have been able to do slightly better—but most minor mistakes can be rectified with time and patience. There are still people, however, who succumb to some awful and massive financial disasters.

Financial disasters occur more often when purchasing investment properties than when buying family homes.

When property mistakes are committed by large companies that have been greedy and naive, who cares? What I hate to hear about is the normal, small-time investor who has lost out due to not having enough information to make smart decisions.

With the availability of finance for investment properties, there has been a proliferation of information—both accurate and inaccurate—about how to make money from property. This chapter will help you to identify scams and maximise your chance of making money from wise investments.

Investment crazes around the world

Before I get into the nitty gritty of property investing, I will share a few examples with you about how property investing has taken off both in Australia and overseas. You'll see there is a pattern forming and you'll be able to identify high-risk and low-risk options. You'll be able to make good sensible purchases compared with the ones that some 'investment specialists' swear could make you a millionaire overnight—in reality the chances are about the same as winning lotto. Sure, miraculous money-making investments can happen, but who wants to take a risk worth potentially hundreds of thousands of dollars? Not you, I hope!

Dubai

Dubai is a truly fascinating example of how the property market can affect a culture and an economy, having grown from nothing to everything in less than two decades. Over the last five or six years, many developers have claimed that Dubai is 'the place to buy' if you want to make money from property. In reality, the time to make quick and huge profits was a long time ago, before the big marketing campaigns, before the press caught onto the craze and before the investment companies saw a niche they could exploit.

Back in the mid to late '90s at a real estate agency in London I had a Dubai-based client. He was living in Dubai yet buying units from me in London. Why wasn't he buying in Dubai? Wasn't it an investment property goldmine? Not just yet. In the '90s, even residents were not permitted to own residential property in Dubai, let alone overseas buyers.

In the late '90s, the Dubai government and monarchy decided they would develop their country using all their oil wealth. They realised they could not do this without allowing property ownership, so they literally turned their economy around in one fell swoop. When my client stopped buying in London and started buying in Dubai, he explained to me why. He was buying right at the time before other local and overseas investors knew too much about it!

There were some risks in these early stages, though, as the changes to the legislation were a rumour, so if you did buy on the new scheme you ran a very high risk that your title might never be approved because Dubai residents were still forbidden from buying property in their home country—the government owned the lot.

As mass devolvement started and the rules were abolished, anyone could suddenly own residential property in Dubai. The buyers of the first residential complexes made a lot of money, but they had also taken a huge risk buying. The country at that point had no housing market history whatsoever even though new developments were popping up everywhere. Not only were there no guarantees that the titles would become available, but also there was a great risk that the developments might not even be completed.

Then there was the issue of funding the high-risk investment. Obtaining a mortgage in the normal way was virtually impossible, so you would be funding this investment opportunity by either having a huge sum at your disposal or by using a property in another country as capital. All very complicated and risky, and hard work for the experienced investor. But when it did come off these investors really did earn their big profits as the area grew in popularity and demand.

Now, I would argue that Dubai is a place like any other: if you buy right, you will be okay—but get carried away by marketers, and you could lose out. When the market and media became aware of these investors making astronomical profits and more exciting schemes were launched, the marketers jumped on board. But by the time the word got around, the risks were low and the big profits were not as easy to come by. This is a sweeping statement, I know, but Dubai is now an established marketplace open to the forces of supply and demand just like anywhere else. So there's less profit to be made, but less risk, too.

Spain

Staring in the '90s, Spain became a popular place for Europeans to buy housing. As finance for second holiday homes and investments became more readily available, developers jumped on the bandwagon and started building huge numbers of houses designed to appeal specifically to property investors.

In the past, overseas buyers had to buy properties with cash but the global trend of easier borrowing for homes opened up this market place. Suddenly Northern Europeans could either increase their mortgage on their existing home (if equity would allow) to purchase another home, or could obtain a mortgage on a foreign property. Many British banks even opened branches in Spain just to make the whole process easier.

Now the floodgates were open and buyers flocked in, demand increased, and developers started a building frenzy. The Spanish government welcomed the investment in their country and failed to see the disaster waiting to happen. During this period, buyers became caught up in chasing their 'holiday home in Spain' dream and forgot to ask themselves the key questions. When they wanted to sell, who was going to buy and for how much?

As like most investment opportunities, if you got in early, there was a good chance you were going to make a profit. Then the craze began and the Spanish government allowed massive oversupply of housing specifically designed for investors, and built too many homes that only foreigners would buy. This was a big mistake. When you have housing that only appeals to overseas buyers it is high risk because global influences such as currency fluctuations can have an impact. What happens if there is no demand from local buyers when foreign investors want to sell?

In the mad dash to acquire an ostensibly safe investment property in Spain, European buyers failed to do their research. Even before the global financial crisis, the Spanish housing market was in trouble because of an oversupply of housing stock that was not attractive or affordable to the residents of the country. Nobody there was asking my all-important question: who is going to buy this place if I want to sell it? If they had, they wouldn't have bought at such exaggerated prices or, in fact, bought at all.

Of course over the next few years, the market will settle down and the oversupply will reduce, but it has a long way to go.

Eastern Europe

To aid struggling communist economies in the '90s, some Eastern European markets opened up to the property-buying world. As with any emerging new market the early days were tough and only the very determined succeeded. Initially purchases were very, very hard to finance—you had to battle huge amounts of legal red tape to buy in Eastern Europe. To make matters more challenging, supply was limited to a few new development schemes and limited established housing stock. Also, sellers at this stage were not used to the selling process as historically homes had been passed down through the family.

If a buyer managed to overcome these obstacles and buy a property, they were able to sell and make a healthy profit. Why? Well, because of the labyrinth of obstacles, supply was much smaller than demand, and newly purchased properties were valuable—these buyers did well. However, as the market exploded with countless new developments priced by greedy developers, naive buyers signed up without a care. Much of the appeal for investors was the idea that, for example, a two-bedroom unit in Eastern Europe was substantially cheaper than in other popular holiday destinations such as Italy, Spain and France.

The important factor to note here is that no matter how cheap the property appears to be, if no-one will buy the property it will become virtually worthless. A 'cheap' property is calculated by comparing a home price in that country with somewhere else—France with Poland, for example. France's housing market has a regular and constant demand by local buyers whereas in Poland the market was limited as the local buyers were not able to buy. So the capital gains these foreign buyers wanted actually were their downfall.

New markets that open up to foreign investors are always going to be fragile; factors such as currency fluctuation, bad press and funding difficulties can have catastrophic effects. The market doesn't just dip, it can die completely for years and years.

On the flipside, these high-risk emerging markets can bring high profits if you time your investment right. In these scenarios, sustainability is the key: sustainability refers to a market that has not only a long-term demand, but a varied demand from different sources. For example, if one buyer group drops off, other buyer groups are still able to maintain a demand, albeit at a reduced scale, but still a demand. If the locals are unlikely to buy the housing created by the boom, the only people left to buy the houses are property investors like you, whose numbers at the end of the housing boom are greatly reduced.

In some very extreme cases, buyers who cannot secure a tenant and cannot sell just walk away—very scary stuff! What was even scarier in the time of the Eastern European property boom was the number of companies that promoted homes in these places as 'investment properties'. These promoters should have added that your investment was for their benefit. Please do not relax and think this does not happen here in Australia, because it certainly does.

Australia

The investment mistakes of Europe and Dubai parallel many Australian scenarios. I have personally experienced a number of classic investment mistakes in Australia, and it is my hope that by sharing them with you I will prevent you from taking the same route.

In an Australian hillside suburb, a developer had designed an absolutely gorgeous gated complex with a pool, great contemporary architecture and an excellent mix of homes that were designed to benefit from the location's impressive views. The complex was in the last part of this particular suburb available for construction.

The homes were predominantly marketed to overseas and interstate buyers. The majority of the homes sold for around $900000 to $1000000 at a time when their reasonable market value would have been around the mid $500000 mark at the most. How did the developer get away with it? They implemented an incredibly aggressive marketing campaign designed to lure investors into making a profit at a luxury location. Luckily for the developers, the buyers failed to research the claims made by the marketers. There is also the possibility that the developer had questionable relationships with the valuers and mortgage brokers involved.

The massive mistake the investors made only came to light after they had bought and paid for these homes. After a while, the buyers discovered that the homes could not be leased out for the rent quoted by the developer—surprise, surprise! Consequently, the owners could not maintain their mortgage repayments, and foreclosures followed. More recently, the majority of homes in this particular development have been re-sold for prices around $400000.

So what went wrong? These developers got the designs and the location right—and, sure, there was no reason to believe that these homes would not appreciate very well in future years, but they certainly were not worth the amount that buyers paid for them. Of course, the locals knew that the asking prices were crazy, but interstate and overseas buyers who hadn't done their research were none the wiser.

Had any of the original buyers asked the question, 'Who will buy this house when we're ready to sell in the future?', they would soon have discovered that plenty of buyers would come forward, but none would pay even half the asking price.

One home I saw recently was acquired by an overseas buyer as an investment property for $550000. Now the buyer hopes to sell it for around $1000000. It has been on the market two years, and if it does eventually sell for the asking price you would certainly think they had made a very good choice and not a bad profit, eh? The truth is that this property was acquired in 1995. If they sell for their target price, their profits will not even have doubled in nearly 15 years! Most Australian homeowners who own 'non-investment' homes would have seen their home value *triple* in 15 years.

These scenarios have a common strand: the majority of disasters befall buyers who do not know the local market conditions and fail to do research or ask the right people those right questions.

Common investment property scams and traps

So what is the most common reason for people losing money through property investment? A lot of it comes down to a lack of thorough research, or a tendency to follow trends without understanding the market. But there is a whole industry out there that is designed to take advantage of this laziness and desire for a quick buck. I hope this chapter will give you due warning about a few of the main offenders.

Hot spots

A hot spot is an area described by property 'experts' or the media as the next big place to buy—the implication being that some sort of profit is guaranteed for investors and that capital growth in percentage terms may exceed other areas. Hot spots are a purely fictional media creation. TV shows, magazines and newspapers love to run articles with the classic title: 'The next property hot spot'. Forget them.

If a suburb has been identified as a hot spot, the secret is out so it is likely demand and prices will have risen already to feed this extra demand. By the time the reports of growth are published, this should be used as proof that this is likely *not* to be the place for a quick profit because the price cycle is likely to be close or at the top! You are usually either too late to benefit from the opportunity to buy cheap and rapidly appreciating stock, or the suburb is being portrayed in a favourable light to get you to buy somewhere that no-one wants to buy (or not for the asking prices quoted).

Hot spot buying is great for the lazy investor. They hear a tip of the next hot spot so they dutifully focus on that area to buy, usually relying on the knowledge that the area must be the latest money-making opportunity because it has been classified as a hot spot.

The logic behind hot spots doesn't work because everyone who invests in property is different—they have different financial circumstances, different views on risk and a different amount of knowledge about the location. The hot spot theory is based on a sweeping generalisation about an area which is why it can be risky. Sometimes the hot spot tip is based on an area where house prices have not risen as high compared with neighbouring suburbs, or some major new infrastructure is planned. The predictions could be right, but if you presume because it has been defined as a hot spot you will make a guaranteed return, you could find you wished you had stuck to areas you knew well. Don't assume a hot spot will make you a profit unless you have done extensive research.

Often very intelligent media commentators who *do* understand property will predict the next hot spot, as well as the possible percentage capital growth that could be achieved within that particular postcode. Great! Well, not really, because there is no such thing as a typical home or typical homebuyer—property is far more complex than that. The council or other experts may be predicting a population increase in the area, and transport and infrastructure improvements may be underway—but none of that means anything to Bruce and Shelia who pay too much for a home for the sole purpose of securing something in a hot spot, or their mates Wayne and Colleen who fall for an 'absolute bargain' only to discover that the reason it is cheap is because no-one wants to buy on that side of town. True, some people will make a financial killing, but that outcome would have been just as likely if they had bought in a suburb that they knew well and that they could keep an eye on.

A real hot spot develops because it is an area, suburb or street that has previously been considered unpopular or always considered the wrong area by the buying market. You take a risk and it pays off because others start to buy there too, the area improves facilities and the prices grow ahead of the area around it.

There's also the posibility that a hot spot can dry up before it even takes hold. The other buyers may never come and the possible improvements rumoured to be happening in the area may never be completed by the council. Before your very eyes it could turn from a hot spot to a sub zero spot. Hot spot implies high profit potential but think about the term 'hot spot'—high temperatures can be dangerous and you don't want to get burnt.

In my experience, the majority of property investment mistakes are linked to buyers trying to join a crowd to buy in a newly identified hot spot. So if a hot spot does tempt you, check it out as you would if it were anywhere else—it could be good, but you could also find it's no better than elsewhere.

Property seminars and investors' conferences

Property seminars and investors' conferences can be a great idea for the novice investor, as they can provide an opportunity to listen to advice, access services and information, and maybe even learn about the Australian property market.

But what are these property experts selling you?

A good property expert will be selling you one thing: a ticket to the show! Don't begrudge paying for it, either—you are accessing all of this person's knowledge and that is well worth the money if the knowledge is useful. The problem occurs when at these seminars or conferences the 'expert' is surreptitiously guiding you toward the investment option that he or she *just so happens to have available*. Lucky you! I bet there are only a limited number of opportunities! Sound familiar?

I don't care how good a 'deal' they have, the instigators of these sales-sessions-in-disguise should be there to give advice only. If they have associations with certain investment products, these associations should be clearly stated to you upfront so you can see their angle. If the experts have the slightest undisclosed opportunity for financial gain from the advice they are giving you, assume that their advice is not independent and not necessarily in your best interests.

Think of the process of researching an investment property in the same way as buying general insurance: do you go with the first quote? No, you don't—you do some research, maybe using search companies to find the best deal; it is all about shopping around. Listen to what the people at the seminars have to say and what they have to sell—it might be worthwhile. But once they reveal the location, price, terms and other details, go away and do your own research to make sure you know what you're getting into.

Property experts

The simple reason for which property experts have sprung up over the last 10 years is that there is money to be made from investing in property—and very big money it can be. But be aware that the people making the money are generally the crafty marketers, and these are the people to avoid at all costs. If you involve a marketer in your property purchase, I can guarantee they will be making more dollars from your purchase than you are!

Anyone can claim to be an expert. Many claim to be experts because they have made a real estate killing and now own 567 rental properties. The fact is that these people could just have the Midas touch and have been lucky—their success doesn't necessarily mean that the model they used, the risk they took or the timing they had will work for you. So watch out for so-called property experts. Some, I believe, are from the UK originally: they do a few TV shows, spend a few years working in real estate and call themselves experts! Fancy that.

Investing 101

If, despite my warnings, you still think investing in property might be the right option for you, there are a few important pieces of information that will point you in the right direction and ensure you stay away from risky or unviable investment options.

Know your market

Even the so-called property experts often fail to point out the most important question that must be answered in order to ensure a property investment is successful is: who is the likely buyer?

Whether you want to sell your property in six months or 60 years, this is the most important question you need to answer, and almost all property investment failures occur when this question is not raised prior to the point of purchase.

Why do you need to care about a future buyer? Although property investment should be a long-term plan, we all know life has this great ability to make financial demands on us when you least expect it. So, you need to know you can sell. If you do sell, will it release the money you invested? Will you make any profit? Will you recoup your expenses?

So investing in housing is all about who will buy it from you and what they will pay in the short term. I'm talking about the short term because that is when paying too much or buying something with low demand will really cause you a headache if you need to sell. But if after careful research you buy a high-demand property, this will mean an easier sale. Even if market conditions are at their weakest a good price is still achievable if you bought in the right area at the right time in the market.

Also remember that just because properties sell for high prices does not mean there is a high demand. High prices are always relative. What are you comparing them to? In an area where most properties sell for less than $500000, $600000 could be big money, but then you notice the block is 40 per cent bigger than average and the home is five bedrooms not four, so for $100 000 extra it is good value.

Remember, in any area you can choose how much risk you want. Low risk means targeting the main housing demand for that area and then sticking to the lower and middle sector of that housing stock. High risk would be buying the most expensive homes in the area with a view to capital gains and medium risk could be the least expensive houses or units but in a 'good' area.

I always suggest you actually visit and take time to get to know an area before you invest in it. Don't just rely on the internet and the newspapers—although this is a good place to start. Pick up a local paper and examine the real estate section, and go to the main property websites such as <www.realestate.com.au>, <www.domain.com.au> and <www.homehound.com.au>.

When using online real estate sites, search by suburb and look at the range of properties available, from the cheapest to the most expensive. Check the suburb median price and check price growth of units compared to houses to ascertain demand in recent times. Also take a look at rental prices, and consider whether your housing type is popular in the area. If so, maybe the capital growth could be good because of high demand.

All this information is out there and you need to be thorough and methodical. Once armed with your research, go to the location because you may decide on a house but discover a bargain unit with a desperate seller.

I've outlined an example below to demonstrate what happens if you do not undertake that basic research.

Recently, on the northern end of the Gold Coast, a number of large-scale apartment developments were constructed in a very smart suburb. There was no problem with the location of the development, its popularity or geography—the area was beautiful and popular with locals. These assets were what the developers focused on. It *must* be low risk—this is a gorgeous area!

It is true that the area the developers chose to build the apartments in was low-risk territory, but there was another problem: the majority of the units in the development were the same price as a decent freestanding home in the same area, and considerably more expensive than the smart townhouses or villas in the area. The area might be gorgeous, but who is going to pay more for an apartment than they would for a free-standing house or a townhouse?

If the buyers of those units and apartments had read this chapter before buying, they would have asked, 'Who will buy these?', and the answer would have been 'Hardly anyone'. Once the aggressive marketing by the developer has ceased, everyone would be buying houses and the unit market in the suburb would be nonexistent. The buyers would have discovered that buying in the development was high risk, unless the price was substantially reduced to compete with and undercut the freestanding homes.

Risky business

Risk is often discussed in the world of property investment, yet when actual property is being offered for sale and targeted at investors the word risk is very rarely mentioned. Risk is the first thing a potential buyer should consider. I can assure you that in all the 'disaster scenarios' mentioned in this chapter, no risk analysis was undertaken prior to purchase. It is important to consider (before beginning your property search) what level of risk you are prepared to take.

Risk in the world of investment property refers to anything from buying an old home without a building inspection and discovering it is riddled with white ants to, in an extreme scenario, buying property from a seller who didn't actually own the property. Sounds crazy, but it has happened.

Paying too much for a property because you fail to research prices is high risk, as is buying in a currently unpopular location with little demand hoping that it will improve. You can attempt to reduce risk by extensive research but always be aware that you could win or lose.

Being a born sceptic when it comes to housing, I have never really been comfortable with high-risk investments. For this reason, I have never benefitted financially from the massive payout of a high-risk choice when it goes right. If you ever wondered how big developers make big profits, it's because they are often prepared to take big risks, and in many cases, they get a big payout for taking that risk.

High-risk investments are about the property long shot. For example, you often hear of developers promoting new areas or new developments in areas that no-one would ever consider living in. In fact, that is the trick: developers buy the high-risk land for a low price at a point when no-one else wants to buy it (and many people are telling them not to buy). High-risk land is a parcel of land without development approval at the time of purchase. The land is usually very cheap because of this and the developer hopes to build and develop the area. Really, they deserve to get big profits because they could have lost it all.

But a high-risk investment has pros and cons. The negative side of high-risk investments is that they often result in huge losses, and you have no-one to blame but yourself if the whole project goes belly up. The positive side is that high-risk investments, when they go right, can give the buyer an amazing return and big money.

High-risk investors win some and lose some. They can win a lot with educated gambles, but an investor who buys a high-risk investment without *knowing* it is high risk generally loses out substantially. Similarly, you need to be very careful of property that is being marketed as very low risk. Is it *really* low risk? You must ask yourself this question before you commit.

So what level of risk are you prepared for? Please consider this: high-risk investments, when identified as high risk *before* they are purchased, often result in either big payouts or big losses; but unacknowledged high risk generally means a massive failure.

Low risk means a safer investment with modest returns, but just as high-risk investments can perform both well and badly, low-risk investments can surprise you and perform unexpectedly well (or not so well).

You take high risk if you can afford to lose money. You take low risk if you cannot afford any disasters—which is the case for most of us, of course. There are grades of low and high risk depending on your chosen property, but if you ask the right questions and do the research, you will know what risk is involved.

Location, location, location

Having decided whether you want to go for a high-risk, potentially high-returns investment or a low-risk, low-to-moderate returns investment, you should start thinking about the location of your new investment property. As you are trying to make money from this scheme, you may think I am going to direct you to a particular type of location: the classic up-and-coming suburb, the regenerated area, the CBD area. In reality, where you buy is up to you and will be dictated by your budget, your personal circumstances and your attitude to risk, and so my answer to the question of 'where' will always be the same: buy somewhere you are comfortable with, and where you would consider living, while taking into account the popularity of the location in the market. If you apply this strategy to your location search, you will rarely go wrong.

Some guidelines about things you should be looking for when choosing a location for your investment property include:

- *A location you know.* Or at least one that is geographically close to your home so you can keep an eye on your investment; this is ideal for first timers.

- *Proximity to the CBD.* In any metropolitan or country area what you need to ensure is long-term demand, so locations close to employment centres are vital for tenant demand and future sales. But keep in mind that new areas considered a distance from the CBD when you buy today can become closer as an area grows, so this can be a good long-term punt as long as you are patient. If you choose to buy that little bit further out in the hope of the city or town's centre growing, you should pay less than existing, more central locations.

- *Population growth.* Areas tipped for population growth can be a good purchase, too. Just ensure there is a genuine and tangible reason for this population growth prediction and your possible investment isn't too much of a high risk.

- *Access to services.* Does the area you are looking at have easy access to the CBD and other popular areas of interest? If not, are there plans to improve the infrastructure? Be aware though that sometimes projected plans do not go ahead.

Having picked an area that will work for you, it's important to note that each suburb can be internally diverse, meaning that one part of the suburb might not be as desirable as another. Internal diversity can be due to something as simple as a main road meaning access to a preferred school is harder or takes the home out of that school's catchment zone. It is also common for one side of a suburb to have lower values because housing stock is cheaper and therefore restricted in its value. There could be any number of reasons for this; for example, it could be a hilly area and one side hardly ever gets the sun, or part of the suburb has poor TV reception.

Only people who know a suburb intimately will get the best buy (or, at the very least, will manage to protect themselves from a costly mistake). So if you are looking at an area you aren't familiar with, get to know it: research it, research it again and speak to as many people as possible. When looking at houses in the area, of course talk to the agents, but also chat to the local shopkeepers and café workers. Even see if you can talk to neighbours of homes you are inspecting. Most importantly, *please* go there in person! I often hear of people who have invested interstate or overseas having undertaken just one brief visit to the property they are buying, or who have never been there at all. That is a dangerous thing to do, so don't complain when it all goes wrong and you wish you had stuck to investing in shares!

Specifications

The location you've chosen will dictate the specifications of the properties in which you could consider investing. Wherever you choose to buy, certain types of properties will be in higher demand than others. Your first task should therefore be to become familiar with the specific patterns of supply and demand in the suburb you've chosen. You will start to see what is popular and what is a good buy by learning about your area, so get involved—don't just sign up for the first house and land package or new unit development without first sampling the market. The safest bet will always be to opt for the housing type that has mass appeal in an area, and also the type that is just tacked on to that component of that market.

You also need to establish what types of houses are popular in your chosen suburb. I suggest getting on the phone to agents and asking what is popular in the area, not only the house type but features associated with those homes. For example, are the popular homes close to a good school, facilities or parks? In urban areas perhaps the units have balconies or parking or are close to certain amenities.

By speaking to a wide variety of agents a pattern will form, just as it will form when you look online. Study the descriptions of the properties for sale in the area you are interested in. What features do the write-ups play on? Doing this, you can discover prime streets being promoted as streets only get noted if they are in high demand in an area.

You need to speak to people to discover the popular features of an area. Once you have worked out what they are, ensure your purchase works around this research. Do keep your findings in perspective, though; a street beside a certain park may be the best street to buy in, but you might find a home cheaper only 400 metres from the park and this could be the best option for you. Be aware of the best features, but don't become obsessed— you have to be flexible to make the best out of your investment.

For example, in a family suburb, freestanding houses with four bedrooms and two bathrooms are usually the most popular choice, and therefore an ideal buy (at the right price, of course). But keep in mind that the five-bedroom, two-bathroom house that's selling for just a bit more could be an even better option, because there will always be someone who will want some extra family space and will pay more for it. Likewise, the freestanding three-bedroom two-bathroom house with room to extend or improve that is a bit cheaper than everything else could be a better buy than the 'perfect' four bed two bath.

This is not so much of a case of thinking outside the box as thinking *around* the box. For example, buying a unit that is priced similarly to the freestanding homes in the same suburb is not a good move. Likewise, a five-bedroom, four-bathroom mansion will be unlikely to grow in value at the same rate as the mass housing stock. This is the case purely because of supply and demand. Demand for mass housing stock is greater because it attracts a large number of buyers, but likewise, if there is a shortage of housing at the top of the market, that shortage could also lead to demand in terms of buyers with large wallets.

In an inner-city or prime beachside area, the two-bedroom apartment or unit may be the main housing stock, but that market could be a little crowded—so consider reasonably priced one-bedders, or look at a three-bedroom unit for not much more. You could also buy two-bedroom units too, but if that market is very well stocked with two-bedroom units, make sure your choice is good value and in the lower price range. This is the key here: if you choose the main-demand housing type within an area, only commit if you can find somewhere 'special' in that housing sector. For example, is it underpriced because of keen sellers or needing work and has value-adding potential?

Location and style are about personal choice and what you feel comfortable with but this must be combined with in-depth research. If you want to make money from an investment property, try to not let your personal choice stand in the way of what your research and the market is telling you. So keep that personal taste on the perimeter as you research, so if you do not know the area you have decided on, *get to know it first*. That way, you will come away with a property that makes you very happy and is a profitable choice for many years to come.

The many methods of property investment

There are many different strategies that can be used to buy and then sell property in order to make a profit. The method that suits you best will depend on your budget, the area in which you buy, the state of the housing market, the state of the economy and the type of property you've bought. The main investment strategies are discussed in the following pages.

Flipping

Flipping is when you purchase a home with the sole intention of selling it straight on. Sometimes flipping can be done virtually as you settle, or even before. For flipping to be successful, market conditions have to be absolutely right, and you have to ensure you have managed to secure the home at a price that is under market value—and that is hard. I mean, would *you* sell a home for below market value? No. People sometimes do sell for below market value, and if you've been the beneficiary of such a transaction, it really is easy money. I have successfully flipped only once, and in that case it was the booming mid '90s. I bought a unit in a new housing development that I knew very well. The developers had nearly completed the site and wanted the few remaining units sold quickly, so they let them go cheaply because speed was everything and they had made big profits on the site already. It was a case of being in the right place at the right time. I bought under market value by about 15 per cent. I re-sold it immediately. I too wanted a quick sale, so I sold it at about 5 per cent under market value, and it worked: even though the buyer had a good deal, I still had a profit. True, I could have held out for a larger profit — but the market could have changed, which was a risk I did not want to take.

Estimating rental income for investment properties

There is a basic guide that you can follow when buying an investment property that you intend to rent out. A $400000 home should attract an income of $400 per week to cover its costs, and a $200000 unit should attract a rental income of $200 a week, and so on. I realise this is only a guide as your mortgage repayments will vary depending on whether you take a 95 per cent loan to fund the purchase or only a 50 per cent loan. The bigger your deposit, the less your costs will be. As a guide investors use this little trick with a $400000 home, for example; if it will only fetch $350 per week, it is likely to be negatively geared and cost you each month. Likewise, if the same house rents for $450 per week, it could be a possible positive gearing option. Of course your personal costs related to the purchase will dictate the status.

Use this method as a guide only. You will of course need to do further financial planning if you do decide to go ahead, but it's a quick method to review of your new house's suitability as a rental property. Watch out for rental scams in housing developments. Some developers will quote a rental income of $400 per week 'guaranteed' for the properties they are selling, but that guarantee may only last for a year or two. Ensure that on the open market, your new house really is worth that amount — you could get a nasty shock when the guarantee period ends!

Buy and hold

The term 'buy and hold' means exactly that: you buy a property with the intention of retaining it for quite a number of years, before selling it on. Usually, this means you will rent the home out to tenants. Obviously, this is not possible if you've bought a block of land, but the principle is the same: you buy now and retain, hoping the capital growth will be good and you can sell when the next market boom hits.

Negative gearing

No, negative gearing does not mean driving your Commodore at high revs in low gears—it means making a financial loss each month on a property that you have bought for future investment. Doesn't sound like a good idea at first, does it? In fact, it can be a very good idea for many people, as the loss you make, or the 'negative' part of this purchase, can be offset against your tax bill.

At a time when everyone is making good money and the economy is strong, negative gearing is a very popular way to buy homes for investment—but it only works if you have a fairly safe income, because the loss you make could vary from month to month, and you may need to cover higher payments if interest rates change. In addition to your mortgage repayments, you could incur further costs including:

- rates
- maintenance
- agents' fees
- mortgage interest.

Still not convinced that negative gearing could be a profitable endeavour? The real reason to consider negative gearing is that it gives you a nice tax break for a few years, and the loss you incur should not be too much. The hope is that you'll make a healthy profit on the home over a period of time, and the profit you make each year in capital growth is money you cannot spend easily, so you are forced to save this amount.

This investment vehicle can work well, but you must be sure that the purchase price is sensible, the rental demand is constant and that you can cover losses in the first few years, or else it can be a financial disaster. If you buy right, not only will the value of the home increase, but the rental income will, too.

Positive gearing

Positive gearing is, as the name suggests, the opposite of negative gearing. In this case, you acquire a property that will make you money on a monthly or annual basis. Tax wise, you can't claim for losses except running costs, so your personal tax will not be reduced much. Your property should supplement your income, so you can't claim for losses when tax time comes around.

Finding a positively geared property is quite difficult, unless a 75 per cent mortgage is required (easier when interest rates are low or you don't need a mortgage) in which case it's dead easy!

A positively geared property means money is made each month after expenses. So if you are one very rich investor who can buy a property outright, then running costs will be very low and rent income will mean a big profit each month. However, most investors need to take out a mortgage and the higher the mortgage in relation to purchase price, the more interest each month. So, depending on rental income the profit could be non-existent or very small. The less mortgage interest you have to pay, the greater chance you have of being positively geared.

An example would be where a mortgage equates to no more than 75 per cent of the purchase price, so there is a good chance of positive gearing and making money each month. But many mortgages are at 80 per cent to 95 per cent and the interest payments often exceed the rental income so to positive gear is very hard for many investors.

It must be noted that your negatively geared home can soon become a positively geared investment because of outside circumstances such as rental income increases and interest rate reductions. Likewise, your positively geared purchase can soon become negatively geared as maintenance costs rise, so you must note that whichever option you select, it can change.

Where to go for advice

Despite my criticism of property experts, I am not suggesting that you should ignore statistics, experts, books and magazines, or that you shouldn't attend property seminars. You just need to supplement the advice you get from them with some easy and sensible research of your own, and ask the right questions of the right people. Many investment companies, property writers and experts are absolutely tuned in to the current market and are telling you the right stuff—but there are many out there that are not. You need to be able to work out who is who.

When researching investment properties, by all means, attend seminars, read books, join investment clubs and so on—but be wary: sign nothing without seeking professional advice, and ensure that the people who run the seminar are giving you independent advice. Many banks need developers to sell huge percentages of their stock prior to getting the finance for the project, so do you think you should be paying top dollar at pre-construction stage? Use this info source as a guide only; check out their products and only commit if it adds up.

Rather than going to dodgy marketers for information, turn instead to some of the following experts:

- *Accountants.* They can tell you all you need to know about tax implications, depreciation, allowable expenses and so on. They can offer totally independent professional advice and their advice is not swayed by you buying anything. So for your personal long-term financial goals plus advice on details on how to structure the purchase in relation to tax liabilities and other financial concerns, accountants are great—but just remember they're not experts on property investment.

- *Finance brokers and lenders.* Listen to their advice about how much you can borrow, how much your property will cost you to own and what your options are. These are the guys that tell you how much you can borrow, but you need to ensure the advice they are giving or products they are steering you towards are right for you as they may make commission based on what you decide. Use at least three separate advisers for a truly balanced view of your choices and don't be scared when comparing products with one adviser to ask which one gives them the best fee.

- *Real estate agents.* Speak to agents based in the area in which you wish to buy. These guys are on the ground, and if you can find a good one, he or she will guide you to the right home if she or he knows you mean business. The agents might be biased towards that particular area, but you will certainly get some supply and demand questions answered. Some of the most knowledgeable people in property are your local agents who have been in the industry for 10 years or more. They may admittedly only know *their* part of the state, but you can only buy in one place at a time!

- *Professional valuers.* Use valuers directly. Ask them questions that put your mind at ease. If you're ever buying in an area that you don't know well, employ one in addition to the banks or developers. This could avoid so many pitfalls.

The simple truth is that you can make money from property now, and I hope for centuries to come, if you get the right advice, assess the risk, research your chosen market and get a feel for the area in which you wish to buy. You will be fine even if your investment fails to show much capital growth at certain times in your period of ownership—it will recover, it always does. So relax. Follow a logical, sensible formula—one that works for you, and ensure it is *you* who is making the long-term profit, not someone else.

Happy hunting!

. . . .

What's the agent thinking?

Agents love investors! Why? Because in almost all cases, the purchase of an investment property is not dependent on the sale of an existing property—the buyer usually already owns a home, and as such has some equity, and is therefore ready to go!

The most common mistake agents make when dealing with investors is pure enthusiasm. This may mean that they quote conservatively on likely renovation costs, or they tell you that you'll be able to pull unrealistic amounts of weekly rental in order to entice you to buy. In my experience, your average real estate agent tends to be the most reliable source of information on your chosen investment property, because he or she will have a huge array of potential properties to sell you and will be in competition with other local agents. Of course agents are trying to sell you something but they do have a vast amount of products to choose from and they will always try to help because, even if you go with a less expensive property, they will still benefit with their commission. They are also aware you can find another agent or go online. The guys to watch out for are those 'investment specialists'—not so much the finance-only ones, but the ones that sell blocks on specific real estate developments—the type of companies that supply 'all included deals'. It sounds great, but all those extras are being paid for by someone and that some-one is probably you—so watch out!

Ready or not

Chapter 7

*Are you really ready to
sell your home?*

Before embarking on your selling journey, it's important to prepare yourself adequately for the stresses and strains such an experience will have. Selling is not an easy experience, and unless you have good reasons for moving and are really ready to sell your home, you might find your experience tainted by your lack of motivation—which can be a real problem for agents and other property professionals. I cannot tell you how many times I would have liked to have sat my clients down, looked them straight in the eye (and, in some cases, given them a quick slap) and asked them these questions: are you *sure* you want to sell? Why do you want to move? Why do you want to sell right *now*, and not in a few months, or even a year? Are you truly prepared for the amount of time and energy selling is going to involve?

Unmotivated sellers are the bane of most property professionals' lives. Stubbornness, unrealistic expectations and complete and utter naivety are traits that strike fear into the hearts of agents everywhere. Think about it: in any industry other than real estate, anyone wanting to sell their product would either agree to a sensible sale price or adapt their product to justify their asking price and attract buyers. *But* not you property sellers!

But it's not just for the agent's sake that you should decide whether you genuinely want to sell *before* you go to market. Motivation is the key to a quick and profitable sale—and I don't mean the motivation of *other* people (such as kids insisting that their parents downsize to release equity to lavish on them, or that they move close by for free childminding). As the seller, *you* need to be motivated to sell—for your own benefit, rather than for others. (I'm specifically referring to those of you who have had your home on the market for years, but all the offers you've received have been 'just a bit low'—and because you can 'never quite find the right house to buy', or you have nowhere to move even if you wanted to! Those very statements are clear signs of a seller who is not ready to sell yet. The strange thing is quite often I notice the seller really believes that they are motivated to sell even though the motivation is often forced on them by other people or circumstances!

The importance of motivation

As a seller, you will be required to put a fair bit of effort in to the sales process. Some of the tasks you'll be responsible for include: considering where you will move when you sell, whether you will need to repurchase immediately or could live in rental properties for some time, whether you mind moving your belongings into storage to allow you to move into short-term furnished accommodation and so on.

You'll also need to collate all documents relating to not only the title of the home but guarantees, warranties, council approval for any structural changes you may have made, any recent valuations undertaken or termite inspections done. You'll then need to show this to a lawyer to ensure no other documents are needed and everything is in order.

You will of course be deciding on who and how you want to sell your home, and potentially interviewing possible agents.

With the home itself, ideally you will be spring-cleaning and making sure it looks its best and is ready for inspections from potential buyers. Inspections do take considerable effort and, along with all the other tasks involved with preparing to sell, vital tasks could get overlooked and the whole process either will result in no sale or the situation just dragging on for months or years. If you stay motivated, there is less of a chance of this happening to you.

Without motivation, you will end up making excuses for not putting in the required effort, and you may even inadvertently put barriers in place that could hold back the deal—which of course means the whole exercise has been futile. I once had a client who instructed us to take her home to auction claiming she was very keen to sell and needed to move interstate. The home had been on the market before with another agent and not sold, so we had long discussions about price. The sellers were aware market value was between $840 000 and $850 000, but they wanted more.

We had an offer of $850 000 on auction day which we thought was a fantastic result, but no, the seller claimed it was not enough and would stay put—so much for needing to move interstate! They had spent thousands on advertising and no sale! A few months later they did need to move and they sold for $830 000 by private treaty.

Genuine motivation tends to help you see the sale situation more clearly. This is not an excuse to sell cheaply, but if all the factors point to a particular offer being actually fair you will see value in that offer as it will allow you to move on.

So it's very important to ensure your motivation is clear from the start.

Andrew's hot tip

Agents and buyers will want to know everything they can about your motivations for moving, so get your story straight before you start dealing with them. If you are staying in the suburb and trading up, or trading down because you no longer need the space, there should be no problems — just tell the truth. But if you're leaving the suburb because you hate it and it is too far from everything, or if you're moving because you and the neighbours would rather share a boxing ring than a beer, you'll need to adapt your story a little.

There are many reasons for selling, but if you were to generalise, you could divide sellers into two groups: people who are in control of their situation and are selling because they want to 'move up in the world', or simply feel like a sea change; and people who have been forced, for some reason or another, to sell. Whether the sale is forced or chosen has important implications for the seller's expectation of sale price, as well as the amount of time it will take them to sell.

Whatever your motivation for selling, be honest with yourself. If your reason for wanting to get out does not make sense, you are probably lying to yourself, and will almost certainly find that your home does not sell as quickly as it could have if you had a clear motivation for selling. There seems to be a clear distinction between really wanting to sell and being prepared to accept your home is worth market value and the sellers who have no clear motivation as to why they're selling. These guys only will sell if the price is right and to them that usually means over market value. I have yet to meet a buyer who likes to pay over market value—have you?

On the following pages I will outline some situations in which sellers might find themselves, and the implications for each.

The forced sale

A forced sale is driven by a necessity rather than choice. It is generally undertaken to solve a financial problem, but it can be necessitated by numerous personal and financial complications, including: divorce settlements where both parties want their money and the option of keeping the house is not financially viable; having bought a new home before selling the existing one; the owner's business needing cash flow urgently; or the bank knocking on the door because the mortgage hasn't been paid and foreclosure is looming. Some of the reasons for a forced sale are discussed in more detail following.

The frustrations of foreclosure

Foreclosure is when a homeowner is unable to make the repayments on his or her mortgage that were agreed to in the mortgage contract. The lender, be it a bank or building society, is then able to seize the property and sell it in order to recover the loan they gave the owner. This foreclosure means, despite the title being in your name, you lose your right to reside there once foreclosure has taken place. When the home is sold by the lender, the original mortgage amount is paid off as well as any other charges and payments you missed. There are also selling costs to prepare the house for the market which will be deducted from the sale. The most frustrating and sad part of this process is the former owner has no influence over the price the home is sold for. The lender does have an obligation to attempt to get the best price, but still you will have no real control.

Financial reasons

The motivation behind many property sales is financial. Home-owners may want to release some equity or reduce their mortgage, or maybe there has been an unexpected emergency and the owner really has to find some cash. All these are good reasons to sell, although they are not always desirable. That said, if selling can release money or reduce stress, don't see a sale as a bad thing, but as a productive solution to an undesirable situation.

Personal reasons

There are a vast array of personal reasons for moving house. Many can be negative, such as bad neighbours, a change in the local environment, divorce or family breakdown. There could also be financial worries or loss of income or a business. These are all rather difficult scenarios, but I always tell folks in this situation that they should view a move as a great new start.

Then there are the positive, happier reasons you may want to sell. You might want to trade up to a bigger home, trade down for an easier lifestyle, move to a new area closer to the beach, or just move around the corner to the block or house you have always had your eye on.

Selling to downsize

Downsizing means selling one home to move into a smaller, usually cheaper, home. Downsizing can make a lot of sense at certain points in our lives, even if it is just for a lifestyle change. The most common motivation for downsizing is when there are suddenly fewer people in the household—for example, when children have moved out of home.

I love working with these 'downsizers' when they are inspecting potential future homes. They often make comments such as, 'Well, it's *smaller* than the one we have now'. Of course it bloody well is! That is the point, isn't it? Comments like this are generally an indication that the buyer's motivation is not strong enough because he or she is not ready to downsize.

The level of urgency in a forced sale could range from 'we need to sell soon' to 'oh my God we needed a sale yesterday!' Of course, the more urgent the sale, the less likely it is that a good price will be obtained. On the other hand, an urgent sale could attract bargain-hunting buyers, so the property might sell more quickly than it otherwise would. These factors have implications for the way in which the house is marketed.

The following are classic lines that you might have seen in a property advertisement online or in the paper:

- 'forced sale'
- 'sellers bought elsewhere'

- 🗩 'bank foreclosure'

- 🗩 'sellers financially overcommitted'.

What do these comments say to you? As a potential buyer, I would personally be thinking, 'Goody, goody! I can forget top offers for this place — these sellers are desperate so they'll accept pretty much anything!' (At the very least, buyers will know that the seller is serious and not one of those annoying market testers, who as the statement implies are literally just doing that — testing to see what price they can get for their house with no intention of selling below their inflated asking price!) So you can see why agents use these tactics to sell properties — they do get buyers' attention — but it's important to consider that comments such as these are unlikely to encourage the best possible price.

Seems unfair but it's true!

On the other hand, if you are a buyer, a forced sale can be a good opportunity to snap up a bargain. The extent of the advantage to buyers will depend on the specific situation — for example, how urgent the sale is, how long the sellers have been trying to sell and any prior offers or failed sales.

The choice sale

A choice sale is a sale that is freely chosen by the seller, and will often have evolved from a strong motivation to sell. The seller will usually have a target sale figure that has been decided on after extensive online research and in consultation with local agents. Some main factors that lead to choice sales are discussed following.

Trading up

Trading up refers to selling in order to buy a property with more space, a better location and so on, and is covered in detail in chapter 5. If the buyer can afford to trade up, this is a very popular option. It's great to see buyers in this situation, as their motivation to sell is to get a bigger and better home. Why wouldn't they be excited?

A new location

A desire to change locations leads many people to sell their home. Countless factors can contribute to a decision to relocate, including a desire to be closer to a new workplace or school, or a lifestyle change such as moving from the inner city to acreage, or from the suburbs to the beach. When selling in order to relocate, you must ensure the new location will give you the type of home you want for a price you can afford.

The lure of a potential high sale price

Price is such a strong motivator, isn't it? Come on, you *know* it is. If I were to approach the owner of a family home worth $400 000 and offer to pay him or her $500 000, the owner would jump at the chance (after protesting a little about their family home being a sanctuary and it not being all about the money, of course).

But the reality is that I'm not going to come along and offer you a price that's way above market value, and neither is anyone else. So before you consider selling, ask yourself this: if you expect someone to pay over market value for your home, does that mean *you* will pay over market value for someone else's home? Clearly, the answer is no. So why do so many sellers expect others to pay above market value for their home? I know one or two of you will have sold real estate for a premium because the land on which your house was built happened to be rezoned, or you had the only home in the suburb with an ocean view. But in 99 per cent of cases, your house will sell for market value, and not a penny more.

Most people work out their target price by going through the following process:

1   Conduct some preliminary online research to determine the sale price of properties similar to yours in your immediate area (see chapter 2 for suggested sites).

2   Ask two or three local agents to inspect your home and suggest a value. If their figures are conflicting, employ a professional valuer to get an accurate figure.

3   Ignore it all. Presume the agents' prices are too low, as they will want a quick sale. Assume the valuer is being too cautious as a valuer can be sued if the amount they give for the property is way over the price when it goes to market. Then, add at least 10 per cent to the price suggested by websites, agents and valuers because *your* house is obviously better in every way than anyone else's!

In all seriousness, remember that a good sale price is a perfectly acceptable reason to sell, as long as you have a realistic expectation of that sale price.

 Buyers beware: choice sellers are often operating on a completely different playing field to you and the rest of the market when it comes to price. Don't be sucked in!

The implications of selling

Generally, the implications of selling are clear: if you sell, you get some money. But there are consequences for the rest of your life, too. These should be considered before you begin the selling process to ensure your motivation is strong and you've considered all the consequences.

Financial implications

Unless the government suddenly decides to start taxing us on the sale of our family homes, there is no tax implication for selling your property. (If the government even *hints* that they might do this, please vote for someone else! Alternatively, get a group together and stage a coup.) There are, however, other costs involved in selling your home. These include:

- 🏠 legal costs
- 🏠 agent fees
- 🏠 selling fees and stamp duty
- 🏠 removal costs
- 🏠 bills to settle and close
- 🏠 buying new items to furnish and decorate your new place
- 🏠 buying new fittings and appliances for your new place if you've agreed to leave your existing ones in the home you've just sold
- 🏠 the cost of preparing your house for the next owners
- 🏠 penalties for paying out your mortgage (if applicable).

Check all these costs out before you sell.

Go online: <www.realestate.com.au> and <www.domain.com.au> both have calculators and guides to moving, buying and selling and their associated costs.

Personal implications

Whatever your motivation for selling, there will be some impact on your life. Hopefully this impact will be positive, but sometimes it won't be—which is why it's important to ensure your motivations are sound *before* your leave a home that has worked well for you and that your whole family loves. Moving house is a big deal, so be prepared: think about it first, and make sure you are comfortable with the impact the sale will have on your life.

Some examples of negative and unexpected personal implications could be that settling into your new home takes longer than expected—the kids might take a while to settle in and everything feels different. In my experience, the longer between moves the harder it can be to settle in to the new home, but hopefully that feeling of displacement doesn't last too long.

Once the deal is done, it's too late to change your mind and another move would be very costly and inconvenient.

It's not all about the money: selling for a loss

On reading that heading I'm sure you are thinking, 'Why on Earth would anyone ever agree to sell for a loss?' Well, besides the occurence of unpredictable and sad circumstances, certain market conditions can make selling at a loss a strangely sensible solution.

People love to claim they bought a place for $200 000 and sold it for $300 000 within two years. But if you look carefully at most people's investment history, you'll find that even the savviest investors have to sell at a loss from time to time. In specific circumstances, selling at a loss might be the wisest move you can make.

Often, selling for a loss occurs when the owner finds himself or herself in a difficult financial position, and selling the home is the only option that will get him or her out of debt. If this has happened to you, try not to be pessimistic about it. In cases such as this, selling for a loss can have a significant positive impact on your life. The worry and stress of mounting debt is very unpleasant, and hanging on to your house in difficult situations may not be healthy financially or emotionally. In difficult scenarios, selling even for loss can at least give people their lives back—and the benefits of that should never be underestimated! By selling, you may be able to halve your monthly expenses. Admittedly, you may lose some of your equity (which is an awful scenario) but sometimes the choice to sell may prevent foreclosure, and your losses may be substantially more if you don't sell.

When it's best to cut your losses and get out — fast!

I have some dear friends who suffered badly in the big recession in the late '80s. They bought a unit at the height of the market with a 100 per cent loan — and why not? Everyone was telling them to get on the property ladder before it was too late. Unfortunately, they bought just as the market started to turn. This purchase meant that for several years they had a mortgage worth more than the home itself. They stuck it out and finally sold the unit at a big loss, and had to take another 100 per cent loan — this on top of the debt from their first unit! This time, they bought wisely on a slowly recovering, very sombre market. In a year or two, not only had they covered their negative equity debt from the unit, they had clear equity in their new home. Within four or five years, they had more than 50 per cent equity in their home. Not bad for a couple who had absolutely nothing but huge debt five years before. Their success was a combination of common sense and good timing. They knew that if they sold their unit for a loss, the bargain they could buy would increase in value and help redeem the debt.

Trading up at a loss

Believe it or not, selling for a loss when trading up can be a good move. For example, let's assume you paid $500000 for your home and now have a $400000 loan outstanding. Your household income is strong and reliable, so you decide to trade up and buy a $650000 home. The market is down, so you can only sell your home for $450000—that's a $50000 loss! Well, not really. The 10 per cent reduction on your sale price is because the market is down, so you'll probably get a 10 per cent reduction on the house that you buy, too. A 10 per cent saving on a $650000 new home means you save $65000, which easily covers your $50000 loss. So there's no real loss, just gain! I have simplified this scenario somewhat, but it is a very common position to find yourself in during quiet or downward market cycles.

As this chapter has shown, if you have a valid reason to sell and have prepared yourself both financially and emotionally for your move, you'll be ahead of the game. Stay motivated and in control, and acknowledge that while you may well earn a healthy profit, at some point in your property-owning career selling for a loss might be a necessity. And if you do want to sell real cheap, just let me know.

What's the agent thinking?

The biggest frustration any agent can have is an unmotivated seller. Feeling unmotivated can mean a seller is less likely to cooperate or take the initiative, and an ambivalent attitude to their decision to sell can mean that deals are often postponed or halted because the seller just does not have a real interest in selling their home.

So, for the good of your fellow countrymen, please avoid selling if you are not really motivated!

Buyers and agents will get tired of your feeble excuses for not accepting excellent offers for no other reason than because you're too busy at work, or because the buyer wants settlement on the 21st and you claim to want settlement on the 22nd and you are not available to sign the paperwork anyway because the car needs a service! We can see through your excuses.

As you might expect, agents love a forced sale. In scenarios such as this, we often get to deal with highly motivated sellers who are prepared to meet the market in terms of conditions and prices.

Ready, set, GO!

Preparing your home for sale

It's confession time: how many of you have listed your home for sale without any preparation, effort or thought as to how you might maximise your sale price, or indeed your chances of selling? Come on, admit it—I know a lot of you are guilty of this. I must confess to being a little jealous of the relaxed attitude of those of you who put your hands up—you are obviously wealthy enough to waste time and disregard the potential of a higher selling price. Lucky you!

I'd like to share with you a story about a time when my family and I had recently listed our home for sale. I returned home from work at about 5.30 on a Friday evening to find my wife, my eight-year-old daughter and my newborn baby perched on the edge of a sofa in the family room. And I do mean *perched*—obviously, they couldn't lie back on the comfy couch, as that would squash the perfectly placed cushions! Not only was my family unusually quiet and sitting in total discomfort, but the entire house looked like a display home. The scene made me feel all warm and fuzzy as they played along with not squashing the cushions, but alas, I knew these were not normal circumstances.

I was not surprised by my wife's response to my queries as to why my girls were acting in such a way and why our house was pristinely clean: our agent had called and advised that a buyer wanted to look at the house within the hour. This explanation from my wife was followed by a barrage of colourful expletives indicating the difficulty both she and our elder daughter had endured to transform our home into immaculate condition in less than an hour—with a newborn baby in tow.

The great news was although this round of buyers were not convinced it was the best buy on the market (the fools!), a buyer inspected the following day and appreciated my wife's efforts and bought the house.

The point of this story is that yes, the preparation that goes into maximising your sales price might be inconvenient, but unfortunately it must be done if you care about how much you will make on your property. Of course, if the market is on fire or you just don't care about how much you sell for, you might be able to get away with leaving your net curtains up, your ute on the front lawn, dirty dishes in the sink, an array of undergarments scattered liberally around the bedrooms and bathrooms and your kitchen bench tops hidden by paperwork, the kids' home-work and aged food particles. But sadly, the market does not always behave in the way we would like it to, and the fact of the matter is that most of us don't have money to waste selling for lower prices.

The analogy I always use when talking about getting your house ready to sell is this: before you sell your car, you check the ads to see what your '93 Falcon is up against. Then you clean it, shine it, tidy it and spray the tyres black. Realising it is actually still quite a nice car, you wonder why you are selling it!

So the question is this: why on earth don't you think to do similar with your house when it's time to sell?

Getting your home on the market involves time, research, effort and usually some money, but the process is unavoidable if you want to get a top selling price. So how do you maximise your chances of sale and high profits?

Following is a checklist that will help you get the best possible price for your home:

- Enlist the help of an agent or professional valuer to give you a rough target price to aim for when selling your home.

- Check out the competition—find out what you are up against. Be honest with yourself about what your home is really like, and what potential it realistically has.

- Decide whether you need to make any substantial changes to your home, focusing on what buyers want and expect for a home in your target selling price range and locality.

- Set a budget for the proposed changes.

- Undertake the changes you've decided on, being careful to stick to budget. Remember to think like a seller and stop 'living' in the house as if it were your long-term home.

- After your changes have been made, have the home reassessed and get it on the market!

Each of these elements will be discussed in detail in the remainder of the chapter.

Establish a rough target price for your home

The first thing to do when trying to work out what, if any, changes you'll need to make to your house in order to maximise your chances of a profitable outcome is to get a rough estimate of the sale price of your house. To do this, it's best to enlist the help of the professionals. You should ask local agents in your area or a professional valuer to inspect your property and give you an estimate of its potential sale price.

Check out the competition

When selling your home, you need to work out what you're up against. The only way to do this is to check out the other homes for sale in your price range and area. In an ideal world, you would personally inspect some of these properties, but that means wasting the seller's and agent's time. For this reason, it is best to view properties online, in the papers and in agents' windows.

Assume that you've sought professional advice, and have been informed that your home is worth $500 000. Having ascertained a basic price guide, put yourself in the shoes of a buyer who might be interested in your home: start looking for homes priced between $400 000 and $600 000, ideally for sale in your suburb, or similar surrounding suburbs. You are the local so you will know if a suburb is comparable or not.

The best resources you can use to make sure your research is thorough are:

- <www.domain.com.au>
- <www.realestate.com.au>
- <www.buymyplace.com.au>
- <www.rpdata.com>
- <www.pdslive.com.au>
- <www.myhousevalue.com.au>.

If your agent or valuer has done a good job and you have an accurate figure, your research will show that cheaper homes are not as good as yours is. If you find houses as good as yours or better for a cheaper price, your target of $500 000 is too high. Similarly, the homes priced over $500 000 should offer more than yours does; if they do not and they seem comparable, maybe your target price is too low!

Pay particular attention to what kinds of features seem to be in demand in the target market. For example, if you live in an established area where the majority of homes are around 20 years old or more, you will probably find that many kitchens in the area are out of date. If yours is, too, you would need to look online at homes for sale and see how many have upgraded the kitchen, and if they have, to what style and standards. Then compare the price difference with the homes that have and the homes that have not. Based on this comparison, you could then decide to leave it alone, do a cheap but effective 'makeover' or even think about refitting the whole room. Not only will this online research help you to gauge the standards of homes in a similar price bracket to yours, but it will also give you some clues in terms of what you need to do to prepare your home for sale.

Be honest with yourself

When analysing your home's saleability, you really do need to think like a buyer. 'Thinking like a buyer' is so important in this context, but I do realise it is very hard to do. Agents and valuers can really do it better than you can, because it is almost impossible for someone with so much on the line to be completely honest when comparing their home to other homes for sale. You live in the home already; you may have built it, renovated it or just loved it for years.

If you get this right, you will know the true market value of your home, and will be in a good position to determine what you'll need to change or improve in order to get the highest possible price or quickest possible sale.

You may have built your double garage by hand using imported Italian bricks; the window may be made from glass that's been hand-blown by South American monks. These features, you think, will certainly increase the value of your home. As hard as it may be, you have to put thoughts such as that out of your mind. Expensive personal enhancements, especially ones from a few years ago, are almost worthless and can arguably lower the value. A double garage is a double garage, and there is no extra value to be claimed just because it has sentimental value to you.

To renovate, or not to renovate?

We have already discussed renovator's delights in detail in chapter 3. This section is designed to help you decide whether renovating is a smart option for you before selling.

Sometimes you will find that there is a substantial difference between your house and other houses for sale in your suburb. For example, you might be living in an older home in a new area, where all the other houses are shiny and new. If this is the case, you may have to undertake some serious upgrades if you want to compete on price and buyer appeal. On the other hand, you might be willing to settle for a lower price than the better homes in your area. Remember: a low price expectation will get a sale for even the most appalling home.

There is a clear doctrine in real estate that will help you decide whether or not to renovate your house. It holds that in an average Australian suburb, around one or two out of every 10 houses will be in a very poor, dated condition. These houses will sell at a low price compared with the others. Conversely, one or two out of every 10 will be in excellent condition, and will be sold at top prices for the area. The remaining six to eight out of the 10 will be average in condition and price. The interesting fact is that the most saleable homes out of this mix are the two out of 10 homes with potential for renovation, and the two out of 10 in excellent condition. Our budget of $30000 for the trust house (see the box opposite) would only have taken it from renovation project to average standard; by keeping it in the renovation bracket, we were able to sell it in a high-demand category and exceed our price expectations.

The lesson here is to know what you are up against. If you can't compete, don't bother; but any effort you put in to clean and tidy the house up (to make it a 'liveable renovation') is always worth doing.

Spend a little or spend a lot?

Let me tell you a story about a client of mine: a charitable trust, which was the sole beneficiary of an elderly man's estate. The man had no family, and the trust had helped him considerably during his lifetime so he kindly willed his assets to the charity. The trust was delighted, and had access to around $30000 in funds to upgrade the home to ensure it would achieve a top price when sold. The members of the board decided to utilise my services so I could direct them in how best to spend their money.

After inspecting the house (which was very old and tired and left a lot to be desired), I took them up on their challenge and started to spend their funds on upgrades. To their complete shock I instigated a total spend of only around $2500 to prepare the home for the market. After witnessing their obvious surprise, I explained why I had done so little despite the money they had available.

This home was around 30 years old and, besides some general maintenance that had been carried out over the years, it was in its original state. To do a complete upgrade on the home with an aim to achieve its full potential value would cost, I estimated, a minimum of around $70000 to $80000. The $30000 available was simply not enough to do a full renovation.

So, instead, I organised to have the front and rear yards tidied, the grass mowed and borders neatened. The inside of the house was cleared of belongings, thoroughly cleaned and freed from old and scruffy window dressings. What this created was an impression that the property was suitable as temporary accommodation while it was being renovated. I marketed it as a 'renovator's delight', and it was snapped up quickly — it actually exceeded its initial projected selling price.

Renovating your home

If you've decided that you need to renovate your home in order to stay competitive in your housing market, there are a huge number of things to consider. See chapter 3 for an extensive discussion of the renovation process. Importantly, you must look at the property as an overall package if you are to secure a buyer and get a good price. This avoids massive overspends and wasted resources, as well as reducing the chances that you'll miss something important.

For example, if your kitchen is very outdated, unfinished or just looks plain awful, you may want to totally replace it—appliances and all. However, you may also need to add new flooring, and the bathroom may need re-tiling. In this context, your big plans for the kitchen need to be toned down: suddenly new handles, bench tops and a good clear out seems more sensible than spending all your money on a brand-new kitchen with a sparkling new set of appliances. This option achieves a good result and still leaves funds for other essentials.

How much should you spend?

The first thing you need to do when preparing your home for sale is set a budget for improvements that will ensure you don't over capitalise. The aim of this process is to ensure you get the highest possible price for your house in the current market.

This process will invariably cost you money. So how much should you spend? You might as well be asking, 'How long is a piece of string?'

Unfortunately, there is no clear amount, or even a percentage of the anticipated sale price, to suggest as a definitive rule. The amount you spend can only be calculated through brutal honesty about the value of your home in the current market, and your ability to sell it.

There are, however, a few guidelines that may help give you some idea about how much to spend. For a home that is less than 10 years old, look at spending around 1 to 2 per cent of its value on improvements. A home of this age should only need a little tweaking—for example, new taps; some new flooring; a few new blinds; a bit of furniture hire and some painting. If your home is old but has been regularly updated over the decades, it can be as easy to touch up as a 10-year-old home—so 1 to 2 per cent of the home's value could apply again.

Homes more than 10 years old are much harder to assess. This is because the amount you spend will depend on the house itself: whether the kitchen and bathroom have been over-hauled; whether extra bathrooms have been added or extensions completed. Even a dated floor plan can be worth overhauling —fashion changes even in the world of home layout, so it doesn't hurt to be up to date. You may also need to spend some money on accommodation if you renovate key living areas in your house.

If modernisation has been scarce, you will need to look at a bigger spend for the home to attract a better sale price. At least 2 to 4 per cent will be needed.

With older 'character' homes, there is the added confusion that leaving an unmodernised home in its original state (and spending nothing) can actually be lucrative in the long run. The reason behind this is simple—unless you plan to modernise in full, the investment in works to the home may not necessarily be returned with a higher selling price. A total renovator is a project ready for someone and cheap; a half-done renovation is not appealing to the market because what has been done so far will be carefully scrutinised by potential buyers. So leave it alone if it is a big project, but make sure you do some clearing out and cleaning as it is cheap and worth doing!

One element that cannot be measured is how much your home improvements will increase interest from buyers. In all my years in the industry, I have learned that correctly undertaken improvements will enhance the home's buyer appeal. However, that buyer appeal is impossible to put a figure on. What improvements can do is attract a buyer sooner rather than later —it could even attract more than one interested party, which tends to create a highly desirable situation where multiple buyers bid against one another, which always pushes the price upwards.

I *can* guarantee, however, that if you take time to assess how to improve your home and then undertake changes as part of an overall improvement package, you *will* benefit.

> ### Working out how much to spend
>
> Assume your home's current value is believed to be around $380 000. Agents believe that a selling price of at least $400 000 could be achieved with some changes. Therefore, if you spend $25 000, you will lose $5000 — assuming that you do indeed get the $400 000 your agent has predicted. You could have spent the money for no reason. In this situation, by keeping your budget to a $15 000 maximum, you would at least have had an impact in the market and got your money back with potential profit.
>
> There is always a 'but' with the housing market. Sometimes market conditions can be very frustrating, and it is not unheard of for people to spend money on their home to improve it, secure a buyer and then end up with less money than they started with. The seller gets all cross because they spent money, and now feel it was all wasted. In reality, if you sell in a buyers' market, the sale price would have been even lower had the improvements not been undertaken, and the sale could have taken even longer had the improvements not been done.

The most important factor to note is to control your budget. If you have been a good little home seller, you will know what you are up against and won't get carried away with an over spend.

The website <www.buildingchecklist.com.au> contains some excellent information that will help you with budgets on renovations and building projects.

Keeping up appearances: the art of home staging

Even if you decide not to undertake a full renovation on your home, you'd be foolish to assume that no work at all needs to be done to maximise your chances of a speedy, successful sale. So, where do you start when you decide to undertake improvements to your property? Is it essential to revamp every room, or is it enough just to update a few of them? You will always hear my fellow experts claiming that kitchens and bathrooms are the most important rooms of the house. Well, that is true—but unfortunately, it's not as simple as that. You can't target those two rooms and neglect the rest of the house if you're keen to get the highest selling price for your home. To prepare your home for the market, you need to think about the overall package you're presenting.

If you are serious about selling and you want to get as high a price as you can in the current market, you need to stop procrastinating and make it happen. I hear so many excuses about why sellers aren't adequately preparing their house for inspection that I could write another book, but I will hold these comments back for another time.

Kerb appeal

'Kerb appeal' is a much-used phrase in real estate circles, and refers to the way the house looks from the street. The way your home is presented at street level is vital to securing a successful sale, whether you live in an apartment building, a townhouse, a freestanding home or semi-detached house. Many prospective buyers will do a 'drive-by' to ascertain whether it is worth attending an inspection, so how your property looks from the street can make or break a deal—no matter how great your place looks on the inside.

As an agent, I love the anticipation of the drive to see a new listing. You travel along in your gleaming Camry down Eucalypt Way looking for number nine with excitement and delight. What will your new listing be like? How will the external photo look? Then you get to number nine and it's ...

Okay.

Or it is *fantastic!*

Just think how different my mindset would be on the day of the inspection if the house is gorgeous rather than just 'okay'. At least, as an agent, I will still bother to show up to a filthy house—a buyer might drive by and think 'forget it!'

The majority of Aussies live in freestanding or semi-detached homes, where you have total control over your kerb appeal. An obvious exception is when you have a neighbour in the street whose home is a shocker—in which case there's not a lot you can do. If the offending neighbour's house has a simple problem that is actually in breach of local council guidelines (such as rubbish in the front yard, or too many vehicles including semi trailers) you may find that the council will help.

When kerb appeal goes wrong

Picture this: a very attractive new housing estate with a main entrance road lined with gorgeous homes overlooking a lake. The homes in the best part of the estate (the section directly overlooking the lake) have a service road behind them so that residents can access their garages without obstructing their view to the front or blocking up the street.

But then, one day, a new owner — who just happens to be a truckie — moves in, with his truck in tow. And, of course, he parks it out the front of his house — not just once a week, but every night and most weekends! How the lovely streetscape has been ruined.

Sorry truckies, but if that is you, imagine how your neighbours feel. Please either leave your equipment at the workplace, or move out to the bush — otherwise you may find that a rather clever but anonymous resident creeps out in the cover of night and lets your tyres down. Shame!

There are a few important things that almost any homeowner wishing to sell should take into account when preparing their house for prospective buyers. Consider the overall look of the home—completing only a few tasks because you're lazy and can't be bothered putting in any effort just won't cut it. You have to be comprehensive and careful if you want the best outcome—no excuses about costs here. It will only take up a few weekends and a few trips to the hardware store to ensure your agents and buyers get excited when they turn up outside.

The front yard is the most important thing to get right, as it will be the first thing agents and prospective buyers lay their eyes on. Think how the home exterior will photograph—even try taking some pictures yourself and then reviewing them to see if it really does look good. Following is a checklist of things to consider when preparing your front yard for inspection:

- Windows should be clean and have modern dressings such as roller blinds, roman blinds or neat curtains tidily placed. With blinds, let them hang down a quarter to a third of the opening.

- Paint colours should be modern and preferably neutral: white, beige, brown, apple green and grey are all up to date. Also take note what is in fashion at the time—visit display homes or buy interiors mags for inspiration.

- Shades or timber finishes are great for garage or entrance doors.

- Mailboxes should be smart and well presented.

- House numbers should be clear and visible from the street. Go for silver or stainless steel with brushed aluminium finish.

- Fencing and gates should be neat, as should the driveway.

- Pathways, lawns and borders should of course be tidy and well kept.

- Don't allow trees and shrubs to hide the exterior completely; people want to see what they are getting, and good planting should frame the home rather than hide it. Use planters and pots filled with healthy plants instead.

- Hide unsightly objects such as rubbish bins and old cars.

- If you have large, ugly, concreted areas, cover them up and put gravel and planters on top—costs bugger all, and the effect is amazing.

> ### But what about apartments?
>
> If you live in an apartment building, how is it possible to alter how the property looks from the street? You'd be surprised how far a little effort to tidy up can go. If communal areas such as foyers, car parks or garden spaces are filled with rubbish, scruffy or need painting, and no-one else will attend to it, maybe you will need to don your rubber gloves and take care of it yourself. Some of your neighbours may help, but don't expect it — in fact, some of them may tell you to sod off! Bear in mind that it is important to seek permission from the building manager before doing any major works (such as painting).
>
> When buyers inspect homes under community titles (such as units or townhouses), the appearance of the surroundings tells them a great deal about how well or how poorly the complex is being managed. It's very easy to lose buyers — no matter how cheaply you are prepared to sell or how fantastic your unit is — due to them being fearful that the complex they are buying into could be a nightmare. A bit of tidying and painting could go a long way.

The inside

The biggest barrier average householders have in selling their home for a premium price is their day-to-day living. Think about this: did you make time before you left home this morning to clear the entrance foyer of your kids' shoes and bags? Did you make the bed with the scatter cushions? Does the spare room still look like a busy, inefficient office?

The secret here is to redesign your home to be able to survive with minimum clutter. This will allow you to easily prepare your home for an inspection with only a few hours notice. You need to *stop* thinking of it as your home, and start thinking of it as a place to sell.

I really don't care how many kids, hobbies or dogs you have. All those elements create mess, and you need to stay focused on reducing that mess if you want to sell your house for the best price. When you go on holidays—even with your kids, your dogs and your granny—you survive quite happily with about 5 per cent of your stuff. So think of this as a long holiday.

Remember to take a holistic approach to your home's presentation—people want to be wowed by your lounge room and kitchen, but that might not be enough; they will expect every room in the house to look fabulous. I have tried to stop buyers inspecting every last room in a house I am showing, but it never works! I've tried blocking the view of the sewage works or talking loudly to drown out the road noise—it is never a success. The buying public are such a bright lot!

There are a few exceptions to this rule, which may allow you a little leeway when preparing your home. An average Aussie home may have two living areas, a kitchen, a laundry, four bedrooms and two bathrooms. At an absolute minimum, you need the living areas, kitchen, master bedroom and at least one bathroom dressed to impress. But that does not mean the other areas can be shockers. Their importance is merely reduced if the other areas tick all the selling boxes.

Ask for advice

To get your interior ready for the market, ask the opinion of your agents and your friends and family. At this point, please choose those you know have some taste and style. For example, if your friend or family member likes china dolls, thinks net curtains or vertical blinds are the height of style and gets excited by leatherette luminous armchairs with cup holders, stay away!

Clear away clutter

Most people have accumulated an enormous stash of useless possessions that they have kept lying around for way too long. You have to get rid of this stuff! If you don't get rid of it, at least put it out of sight.

Clearing away the clutter becomes even more important if you have an open-plan space, because you will probably be able to see *all* the living spaces, as well as the kitchen, at the same time. That means that if you have an open plan home, you'll have to be meticulous about the lot!

 If possible, store some of your clutter in a storage facility while your home is up for sale; it is not expensive, and it is a great idea for excess furniture and big items such as caravans or boats.

What if my house is small?

If you live in a small house or an apartment, I'm sorry to say that you will have fewer corners to cut. The whole place has to look fabulous and uncluttered if you are wanting a good sale price. Even the rule to leave kids' rooms and laundries untouched doesn't apply if you live in a two-bedroom unit, and bedroom number two is a kiddie mess. In this case, you may have to rearrange it as a normal bedroom. Normally a one-bedroom or two-bedroom home is unlikely to attract buyers with kids; I know — a right pain, but it's most likely that your buyers will not have children yet , so you get my point. It's about adapting to your buyers' demands.

What do I do with my old furniture?

Let's be honest here: we all have old furniture — worn and tired sofas, and so on. It may be great for day-to-day living, but when you're preparing a property for inspection by prospective buyers, old furniture just gives the wrong message. I realise this may sound ever-so-slightly mad, but successfully selling your home is all about creating an impression. Many pieces of your existing furniture can look much better if they are cleared of clutter, or improved with new cushions or new covers.

Hide very tired old pieces in the garage or storage facility — but be careful to make sure that the space created doesn't feel like a void. If it needs filling again, buy, borrow or hire something more stylish: these days you can hire literally anything, including pictures, mirrors and even vases!

Take photos to check your work

When you have cleared your clutter, removed offensive pieces of furniture and redecorated your home, check your work by taking pictures. These days, the majority of sale leads will come from the promotion of your home online, so it's important to get as many interested buyers as possible through this medium. As the first thing potential buyers will learn about your house is the pictures they see online, it follows that the better your pictures, the better your chance of selling and getting top dollar.

Good pictures are down to a good camera and good photographer, and no photographer does a good shoot on your home without you giving them a good room to photograph. So take pictures and review them based on the following checklist:

- Is there a weak feature? A weak feature could be something that dates an otherwise quite modern home, such as light fittings, old air conditioning units or a dated dishwasher. Often these issues are easy and cheap to rectify, but if the replacement is too costly could you get by just removing the offending item while you're taking the pictures?

- Are there elements you could easily improve? Stop complaining about minor unfinished jobs and just get them done—the knock in a wall, the broken door handle, the scruffy outdoor area—all can be easily improved and will not go unnoticed by potential buyers.

- Should you move things around? When you look at a room, or the picture of it, does it look balanced? Are there any obvious empty spaces? It is a misconception that an empty room looks big, as it often is the very opposite. Also be careful not to over-fill it either—think balance.

- Would a mirror or picture fill a gap? Mirrors and black and white prints and pictures are popular because they are a safe bet and usually tie in with the scheme of the room.

The pictures taken of your house are your biggest selling tool so make sure the contents are right.

What do I do about my backyard?

The backyard may seem less important than the rest of the property, as it is often seen after the front and the inside of the home. This doesn't mean you should neglect it. Try the following tips:

- Make sure you tidy up. Families with children should always ensure that kids' stuff is not spread across the yard.

- Mow the grass, and ensure the lawn is clean. The worst offenders here are dog owners: *please* no dog poo *ever*!

- Prune bushes and plants.

- Ensure the clothes line is not covered in clothes, and if it folds up, ensure this is done in time for the inspection.

- Hide bins so that they can't be seen (or smelt).

- Ensure fences are well maintained and freshly painted. A new coat of paint can be achieved in an afternoon and you'd be surprised at the difference it can make.

- Tidy up borders, do some weeding and add some new plants for good measure along with a healthy layer of mulch or bark.

- A plain exterior can be lifted by great planting but try to avoid total plant coverage of the building because buyers do want to see what there are possibly going to buy!

- Unless you have a large block or they are very well hidden around the side of the house, caravans and boats should always be taken off-site when you are planning to sell.

Style tips for home decorators

As we come to the end of this chapter, you might still be hoping that I'm going to give you some style tips: what the latest colours are; what wallpaper styles are in at the moment; what type of sofas you should use to dress your home; what style of kitchen; which tiles to select for the bathrooms.

But just as I cannot be exact about how much to spend on your house to prepare for sale, it is impossible to give you cookie-cutter style tips—because I don't know exactly what your home is like. Having said that, let me offer a few suggestions:

🏠 Ascertain your buyer profile and target their likely style and tastes. One of the best ways to do this, if you know your area, is to think about who has moved into your street or area recently. Are they young or old, couples, singles or families? Also, if you invite agents to evaluate your home, ask them who the likely buyer group will be.

🏠 Be conservative, but not to the point of being dull. A common mistake is stripping the life out of a place. Keep some family pictures and some evidence of life such as books and magazines. Totally bare walls can give the home a rental look and conveys to a buyer, if you do live there, that you don't feel like it is a home.

🏠 Do some research for inspiration: have a look at some interior design magazines. The most popular titles are *Better Homes and Gardens, House and Garden, Home Beautiful* and *Vogue Living.* Also look at display homes, interiors of homes for sale or ideally look to the style of sold homes.

🏠 Paint shops are a great source of information. They will be able to tell you what colours are popular, and they'll also know what the latest trends in interior decorating are.

Because home staging (the practice of temporarily turning your house into a display home) is no longer a new phenomenon, it is likely to put potential buyers off. If you 'over-stage', it will be obvious, and buyers will just feel like they are being sold to. (*We* know they are indeed being sold to, but it is a feeling that we don't want *them* to have.) Buyers must feel that you, the current owner, do enjoy the home and its lifestyle—so be aware!

What about rental properties?

A question I am often asked is, 'How do I prepare my house for sale if it is currently being rented by tenants?'

To get this one right, you have to put yourself not only in the mindset of a potential buyer, but also in the mind of the tenant. Failure to do this can really hamper a sale, because tenants are paying to live in the home, not help you sell it, so it is important you see it from their point of view too!

The tenant has legal rights, which will vary from state to state. Of course, because Australians are mad, tenancy law is different in every state. (It drives me crazy!) You must adhere to the standard regulations relating to the selling of your property when you have a tenant in place. To find out what your obligations as a landlord are, consult with your state Office of Fair Trading.

But legal obligations aside, if you act with the tenants' interests at heart, you will understandably find the tenant a lot more cooperative. Imagine being a rent-paying and respectful tenant who had never caused problems for your landlord. How annoying would it be to have the owner expecting continual access to the house to facilitate inspections?

An ideal scenario for many sellers is to allow the tenancy to expire, and prepare the home for sale when the house is vacant. A vacant, tidily presented home will appeal more to potential buyers than a home that is tenanted and dressed for living in. Selling the house while it's vacant could give you the time and space you need to really make the most of the home's assets. This could therefore result in a higher selling figure, which in the long run could be more than the rental income lost in the process of preparing the vacant property.

However, for many landlords, this is not necessarily a viable option. If you choose to keep the tenants in the house while preparing it for sale, there are a number of issues that relate specifically to the situation of selling a tenant-occupied rental property.

Presentation

The presentation of the house is virtually impossible to control if it's occupied by tenants. You may decide to upgrade fittings with tenants' approval, which may add value. But some elements are under no-one's control except the tenants (and, to be fair, they *are* paying to be there). These include tidiness, day-to-day cleaning, whether the beds are made, whether there are undies on the floor and so on.

Access

Regarding access, tenants have clear legal rights to enjoy an undisturbed tenancy. Check your tenancy agreement to clarify your exact rights as a landlord. Usually you will have to follow a clear process of notifying tenants of your intention to sell and then serve notices to inspect. If you have a property manager, speak to him or her before you do anything, or if not, contact your state Office of Fair Trading. If you have a good relationship with the tenant, you should limit inspections to certain times and dates to avoid excess disturbance. Some landlords have it in their stubborn brains that because they pay the mortgage and their names are on the title, the tenant is of no importance. Many landlords who think like this will discover very unhelpful tenants and could find themselves in legal trouble, too—and really, wouldn't you be unhelpful? If you want tenants to cooperate in making your property as saleable as possible, work with them rather than against them.

If you cannot afford the home to be vacant while marketing, don't be scared to offer the tenants an incentive to keep the house tidy. This incentive can be a reduced rent for the marketing period (although limit this time, or they will do all they can to ensure it takes two years to sell!), or perhaps a discount once a sale has been achieved. Ensure inspections are discussed in advance so the tenant does feel involved and in control.

Open days and inspections

Once you have prepared your home for sale, take some pictures and use them to inspire you to maintain a high level of presentation every time you show your home to prospective buyers.

Ensure you have a way of getting your home ready for that short-notice inspection. If you work and your agents have a key to your home, get up extra early and make sure the house is clean and everything is perfect before leaving—just in case.

For inspections and auction days, here are some tips that will help you to showcase your home's best elements:

- Use lighting to great effect. Background lights should be on, and dimly lit areas should have lights on.

- Make sure everything smells good. Use scented candles if it is safe to do so.

- If you have an open fireplace, light fires in the winter; it adds atmosphere and warmth and is always seen as a positive by buyers.

- Use the air conditioner in the summer to ensure your house is comfortable to be in.

- Leave a few photos and magazines around the place— a little evidence of daily life will stop your house looking too staged.

The marketing of homes has become more and more advanced as buyers become savvier. They will know all the tricks of the trade by now, so avoid the following clichéd marketing tactics:

- Baking bread (so '90s).

- Setting the table for a dinner party (so TV makeover—I should know!).

- 📻 Leaving decorative plates containing random pieces of fruit scattered around.

- 📻 Leaving classical music playing on the radio—this is just too obvious.

- 📻 Brewing coffee in the kitchen—please no! This little trick has been so overused it would probably put potential buyers off!

. . . .

What's the agent thinking?

Agents love a well-prepared home. It tells them you are serious about selling, and that you understand that some effort is required. This gives the agent confidence that their clients are more likely to buy.

A well-prepared home may also allow the agent to quote a higher sales figure than they would for a badly presented one. That makes sellers happy and the agent more popular.

Agents will also always notice if you have embarked on a little 'house staging' and got it wrong, and may not be so generous with a selling figure. So watch out!

The perfect match

Chapter 9

*Finding the right way
to sell your home*

As with most things these days, choosing someone to sell your home for you is a little more complicated than you might expect. If you are older, you might recall the days when you were able to order a coffee and the selection was either black or white, with sugar or without—nice and simple. Today, a simple request such as this will be greeted with a barrage of enquiries: what size container would you like? Would you like your milk frothed in a specific pattern? Do you want sprinkles on top? Do you want full cream milk, a bit of milk in your milk, or no milk in your milk? Or, as an alternative to milk—because you do need some more choices—would you prefer this white liquid made by squeezing some rare tree trunk that can only be found in a forest deep in the heart of Venezuela?

The world of real estate is just the same. You can now choose the traditional agency (either franchised or independent); discount or low-fee agencies; you can sell privately (yourself); or you can

179

even use a new breed of internet-based selling services all vying for your money. This chapter should help you to unravel some of the mysteries of the endless choices available to you.

Traditional real estate agencies

Soliciting the services of a traditional real estate agency is still by far the most common method of selling a home in Australia, and to be honest it's probably the best. If you do decide to take this route, there are several factors to consider; these are discussed following.

Agreements between seller and agent

There are several different types of agreements that can be made between a seller and an agent. These agreements dictate the level of flexibility each party has in terms of pursuing alternative options for selling, such as a private sale occurring or going with another agent during the period of the agency agreement. For any real estate agent to be appointed, an agreement must be signed by both the seller and the agent, stating clearly the charges and when those charges apply—it is 'an appointment to act' on the seller's behalf, and that appointment can take various forms. Throughout our fair land, each state and territory will have standard agreements. It pays to familiarise yourself with these forms before signing with an agent. Ask an agent to give you a blank copy to study, or download them from your state's real estate institute. The most important part of your agreement will relate to the obligations you both have in terms of the provision of service and remuneration. The three main types of agreements you can enter into with the agent are discussed following.

Open or multi-listing agreements

If you agree with an agent that your arrangement is 'open', you and the agent have both agreed to a condition in your contract that states that a fee will be paid to the agent only if he or she personally sells your property. This leaves you the freedom to sell privately, or via another source or even another agent, without concern. This type of agency appointment is the most flexible of all as you can terminate at any time or can call in other agents at the same time (and have another agreement with them, too).

If you happen to tell a colleague about your home being for sale and this person buys it, you pay the agent nothing; but be warned, if that colleague has inspected or conducted any negotiations about the home with one of your agents, that agent could pursue you for a fee, even if you actually conclude the deal without involving the agent.

Be aware that in the case of an open agreement, agents are rarely as motivated purely because they could spend their time promoting the home and undertaking inspections only to discover another agent pips them at the post. Another situation can arise where one buyer happens to contact two different agents and sees the home with both agents—it does happen and can get messy and two agents could then be chasing you for fees! Also, buyers can sometimes perceive homes listed by numerous agents as being difficult to sell (presumably for a reason).

An advantage of an open agreement is that more agents are working on your behalf and in competition to get your place sold.

Entering an agreement with multiple agents is not suitable for auction sales, and you do tend to find agents reluctant to undertake any costly promotion at their expense due to the increased risk that they may never receive a fee.

Sole agency listing agreements

A sole agency listing means that you've made an agreement with your agent that they are *solely* responsible for selling your house—they are the *only* agent working for you. A private sale can still be undertaken without the agent imposing penalties on you, but you can't hire another agent. This appointment to act is usually for a set period of time (with the option to extend) so ensure you are happy with your choice. The agent knowing they are the only one should give them motivation that they have something unique to offer buyers. Agents will be aware you can sell to anyone providing that party has no links or communication with the agent. Still the agent could claim they introduced the buyer and you would still have to pay their fee, so tread carefully.

This sole agency is not suitable for auction sales again because you could possibly sell the house from underneath them. However, advertising and promotion are more likely to be undertaken by the agent, as they are the sole agent promoter. They will still want you to pay for most of the marketing fees although 'feature' positions on online property sites or some promotion costs could be refunded when the home sells and that agent receives their fees.

Exclusive agency agreements

You can make an agreement with the agent whereby the signed agent is the *only party* that can sell your property during the stated term. In a case such as this, if your neighbours rock up and tell you their long-lost relatives want to buy your home because it is next door to them, the agent will still want his or her fee. Similarly, if another agent approaches you with a buyer during the 'exclusive period' all you can do is refer them to your appointed agent. Agents appointed this way should be highly motivated and it will make your life easier as any questions you may have you will direct to one person. Because of the nature of this appointment auction sales are always conducted this way.

One of the main issues with exclusive agreements is the length of appointment. Most appointments are of a 60-day duration, but what if, after 10 days, it is clear you guys are not working well together, or you feel they have failed you in their level of service? It can be a tricky situation—see 'What if the agent doesn't perform?' later in this chapter for tips on dealing with this type of situation. I would suggest if signing with an agent for a sole or exclusive appointment that you ask for details of their complaints procedure so if things go awry you know how to proceed.

If you're ever unsure with an agency agreement or appointment, run it past your lawyer. And do ask the agent questions —remember, you are the customer, so make sure you get what you want.

How much will I have to pay?

The fee structure used by agents when charging for their services is quite different from the structures used by other service providers. Generally, you pay the agent a percentage of the final sale price of the house, and this fee includes a number of basic services. Additional 'extras' that are added onto this fee could be: advertising in print media; features or larger-than-normal postings on property websites; for sale boards with pictures of your home; professional photography; and floor plans. Keep in mind that everything is negotiable so do not be scared to push for extras to be included or fees to be reduced.

In Australia, real estate agents usually receive between 2 and 3 per cent of the final sale price of the house. Note that this commission does not include GST or the extra services previously mentioned. This figure can vary hugely depending on a number of factors, including:

- the local regulations in the area
- the quality and success of the agency
- the type of agreement you have with the agent (you may be able to negotiate more if listing on an exclusive appointment)
- whether the property is located in a metropolitan or rural area
- the final sale price of the property (there is usually more room for negotiation the higher the sale price)
- competition between local agencies.

Is it okay to negotiate?

On hiring an agent, you will be provided with a clearly stated fee structure. As a client, at this time you should be free to negotiate with agents about fees. But be aware that if you negotiate too much, a good agent could walk away or become unmotivated. The time to negotiate is when the sale price suggested by the agent at the end of a sales process is much lower than the price they originally suggested when they first valued your property. If they manage to sell your property at the price you originally agreed to, and you are happy with their service, you should pay them based on the originally stated price.

Give the poor old agents a break!

When you complain about agents' fees, remember that agents only charge you when they sell your home — they do not charge for the advice they give you on your home's value, or to show you around 16 homes (none of which you buy). They do not charge you to market your home for two months when you just change your mind about selling in the end — you get my meaning. It all balances out, really, and the sales process would be very challenging if agents did not exist.

As most agents' fee structures are percentage based, it may be more reasonable to negotiate harder when your home has a higher value. An agent has to work just as hard to sell a $300000 home as he or she does to sell a $1 million home, yet, assuming that the fees are 2.5 per cent of the final sale price, their final revenue would be $7500 for the cheaper home compared with $25000 for the expensive one. That's quite a difference for doing the exact same job, and that is a common cause for complaint from sellers. So if you are selling your home for more than $500000, I believe it is reasonable to negotiate with the agent on fees. My fellow agents will disagree, of course!

What services are included in the fees I've paid?

Although the exact level of service you receive will depend on the area in which you live and on the particular agent, fees generally cover services such as valuation, initial consultation, some advertising and marketing, open inspections, basic 'For sale' board, paperwork and all negotiations. Find out what you can expect in the following pages.

The quick sale

A classic scenario that drives me mad is when the client employs an agent and agrees to a marketing price. When the agent's marketing campaign manages to sell the home in a day, the client says: 'That was money for old rope! They hardly did *anything* for their fee!', or 'We must have underpriced the home; the agent just did it to get a quick sale!'

In most of these situations, the agent just did their job incredibly well — he or she got you the result quickly and painlessly, yet you complain. Rarely, it may be true that an unscrupulous agent has undervalued your property, or had a buyer waiting in the wings, but if you were happy to go to market at the agreed price and you had done your research, this is unlikely. In 99 per cent of scenarios, you will only ever agree to a sale price that is too low if you have not done your research and have only listened to one dodgy agent!

Valuation

A valuation is an estimate by the agent of the value of your property. This service will generally be included in the fee you pay the agent when your house is sold. A valuation should be an educated estimate based on recent sales, current market activity and current demand combined with the perceived marketability of your actual dwelling.

If you receive an offer for your property that is lower than expected and your agent is trying to persuade you to accept the lower amount, you can always ask him or her to compromise on the fees. It's always worth a try! Obviously this only works when the value of your property is sufficient to ensure the agent still gets a worthwhile fee.

Before I begin a discussion of valuations, let me clarify something: *valuations are an art rather than a science.* Although there are many methods for calculating property values, estimating for residential properties is often a matter of personal opinion rather than fact. When dealing with commercial, business or industrial properties, it is slightly easier to produce an accurate estimate. The reason for this is quite simple: two identical homes next to each other on the same block with the same specifications will be managed and presented in their own unique ways. One may be presented like a display home, while the other has a more lived-in look; then, when the homes go to market, one seller may be highly motivated, while the other is just testing the market. (See page 211 for a detailed description of testing the market.) This is where the confusion starts, as the lived-in home should be the lower priced, but if that seller is not motivated for sale, both homes could go to the market at similar prices.

How accurate are valuations?

I recently had a client who wanted to sell her investment property. The market was a little fragile at the time, so we decided to have the place inspected by five local agents. I believed the real value of the home to be between $500000 and $525000, starting at the higher expecting to achieve the minimum plus being a little hopeful. Am I breaking my rule here by testing the market? Not really, because the gap between what I believed to be a real value and the maximum suggested the asking price was close. When the five agents submitted their valuations, the figures ranged from $510000 to $635000.

Two of the five agents were from the same agency (although they worked in different offices) and their valuations were $60000 apart! Now, I know I said that valuation is not an exact science — but *please!* This is why it pays to research and have an idea of a real value so you can avoid being misled. As it turned out, the home ending up selling for $515000.

This goes to show that not only can there be a huge discrepancy between different valuation figures, but also that often an agent's valuation can be much higher than the actual sale price of the house.

Agents often have different attitudes to suggesting figures to sellers. For example, one agent may be fair and sensible, and have an excellent knowledge of the local area and the current market. This agent may value your house at $380000, but suggest trying a price of $400000 to allow room for negotiation. Another agent may be desperate for listings, and might tease you with a suggested figure of $425000 knowing full well that this price will never be achieved—but it gets your listing for him or her. An agent such as this will hope that he or she can convince you to reduce the price in time for a sale. Then there are agents who are just plain daft, and who haven't done their research. These agents might suggest $350000 or $450000 because they spent no time researching the market or getting to know your home. For tips on spotting these dodgy agents, see the discussion on pages 223 to 225.

There are a few things you can do to ensure you get a more accurate figure. These include:

- Take on your own research to get a better idea of what similar homes in your area sell for.

- Ask all the agents who give you an estimate to qualify their figure: what is the price based on? What evidence do they have that it is a reasonable figure?

- Keep in mind that most sellers and agents are being too ambitious with their estimates.

🏠 Ask the agents if they currently have clients who may pay the price they have quoted for your home.

🏠 If they do sell the home at the quoted price and a buyer employs a valuer, it is likely the valuer's figure will be close. High pricing now could be a waste of time, as a buyer can be scared off if the home they have agreed to buy is considered 'overpriced' by a valuer.

Andrew's hot tip

The biggest mistake sellers make when selecting an agent is to go with the agent who quotes the highest figure at the valuation stage. Agents know that people do this and play on it, so do not fall for it. You could have valuation estimates from 56 agents, but remember: they are all selling in the same market — while there will be variations between the figures, they should be minimal.

Marketing

The fee you pay the agent will include some marketing services, such as taking photos, writing advertising copy and maybe some limited placing of advertisements for your home in local papers and magazines. Also included will be basic entries to the main property websites such as <www.realestate.com.au> and <www.domain.com.au>.

Print versus online advertising

Should you still bother with print advertising in these modern times? At the point of writing this book, the answer is still 'yes'. Print is still an important part of any marketing campaign, as buyers have not stopped reading the property supplements or classifieds when searching for a home.

That said, online advertising has overtaken the print media in terms of the number of potential buyers reached, so most agents will focus a lot of energy on this medium.

The amount of included marketing varies so much from agent to agent and is impossible to quantify. In general the listings I've mentioned above are about all you get included unless you can negotiate a deal with the agent to split costs once the property is sold. It really is worth trying to negotiate splitting fees if you can, but local agents may just say no—so you have to decide if you feel they are still worth employing.

Before you agree to any advertising spend, always ensure you are being charged at cost and getting the benefit of any discounted rates the agency receives. If you decide to spend more on advertising with the agent, ensure you know where the adverts will appear and when, what they will say, and ask to see results from these publications to know if they really work. The agent may suggest an advertising schedule, and if you run with it feel free to monitor the response, so if it isn't working you can review your options rather than just carrying on spending!

Floor plans

In some cases, it can be worthwhile considering paying for some extra services (that are not included in the agents' fees) when marketing your home. One of these additional services is floor plans. A floor plan is a diagram showing the layout of rooms on each floor of a building. I personally love floor plans, and believe that every listing should have one. By having a floor plan to accompany your listing, you can avoid so many pointless inspections by weeding out buyers who are not going to be interested. Buyers love floor plans, because no amount of words can describe a layout as well as a picture; with floor plans, buyers can immediately decide if the layout works well for them. These may not be as costly as you think, maybe $100 to $200. Some photography companies even offer this service as part of a package. Your agent will no doubt have regular companies they use to draw floor plans.

Ensure you are happy with the internet entry the agent puts together for your property. A successful online ad will have a clear and appealing thumbnail photograph that shows off the home's best features, a snappy, compelling summary of the home's features, use language and terminology designed to target the specific buyer market you're trying to appeal to, and clear instructions about who to contact for further information. I recommend thoroughly scrutinising your entry, as the level of appallingly bad write-ups, pictures and general misinformation agents submit still shocks me.

It also pays to clarify how many sites your home will appear on, because it does make a difference. For example, Sydney buyers mostly use <www.domain.com.au>, so if you are selling in Brisbane and you are only listed on <www.realestate.com.au> a buyer located in Sydney may not see your home online. The same applies in Brisbane where <www.realestate.com.au> is more popular. You need agents who use many different sites for good coverage. Also remember that, for a fee, agents can upgrade your ad and list it as a 'feature' or in a special top spot on the websites; talk through these options with your agent before you decide if that is the best approach for your property.

Open inspections

As part of the service provided by the agent for the fee you pay, the option to hold open inspections will be offered. An open inspection is your home being advertised open to inspect for potential buyers, usually for a period of 30 to 60 minutes once or twice a week with one of these times during the weekend. This is of course in addition to any buyers inspecting by appointment.

Open inspections are a very popular way of drafting buyers: you state the date and time, and the buyers (hopefully!) arrive. Open inspections are helpful in assisting you to get the highest number of prospective buyers through your home, thereby ensuring you get the best possible sale price.

Often, buyers are not keen on attending inspections with the owners present, because it limits the buyers' imagination. They will spend all their time being polite and not really looking at the home. So it might make sense to make yourself scarce on the day of the open inspection. An agent will do a better job on his or her own, because he or she will have an awareness of a buyer's general wishlist, and so will be able to have discussions about possible future changes.

Andrew's hot tip

If you want to hold an open inspection but are too stingy to pay for promotion in the local paper, check out other homes for sale in your area. Find out the times, and tie in with them and add an entry to your website listing saying 'open' and the date and time. This amendment to the site entry is free for the agent to do, as is the agent placing his or her 'open' signs on the street (although check with council first). People who are inspecting the other houses will see your place and pop around. Good idea, eh?

An alternate option to open inspections is the 'by appointment' method. Here, an agent can try to filter the buying public to avoid the purely nosey, possibly criminal and unmotivated buyers.

There is no right or wrong answer to the question of whether to hold an open inspection, so consider the pros and cons.

Pros for the open inspection:

- they provide cheap publicity

- they are usually accompanied by promotion in open house listings on the internet and in print media

- they encourage buyers to have a look, with no barriers

- buyers that attend may see others looking, which will encourage a feeling that the home is popular—and that maybe they should submit an offer, sooner rather than later

- scheduled inspections are easy to work around for busy home owners.

Cons for the open inspection:

- inspections can attract time wasters, just noising around your home with no intention of buying

🏠 the agent may have more to gain from an open inspection than you do, as he or she can meet more potential buyers and sellers to add them to a database

🏠 there is a risk of compromised security. (To minimise this, lock away valuables and paperwork just in case. If many people are expected to attend the inspection, a second agent should attend. Try to minimise the number of entry and exit points so the agent will find it easier to manage.)

The wonders and woes of property photos

When prospective buyers are searching for houses online, the first introduction they will have to your home is often a tiny thumbnail photograph. The quality of this photo can mean the difference between getting a sale and not getting a sale. All agents will photograph your home as part of the cost of hiring them, but the quality of their camera and their ability to take marketable shots can vary wildly, from perfect framing and blue skies to skewed perspectives and an overcast background. I'm sure you've seen examples of both.

The photographs that appear in the advertisements of your property, both online and in the print media, are one of the most important tools you have when selling your house, so it's essential that they are the best they can be. These days, buyers expect great shots of not just the outside of your home — they want lots of good pictures of the interior as well.

Professional photographs are an added extra that, in my opinion, are worth the investment. Without them virtually no-one will know what your home looks like in its best light. Poor-quality pictures taken from weird angles are pointless and will result in complete disinterest from buyers.

Before having photographs taken of your house, you will need to prepare your home in much the same way as you would for an open inspection (see chapter 8 for further details). In addition, I recommend carrying out the following specific tasks before the photographer arrives:

▲ Put the seats down on your toilets.

▲ Remove the magnets from your fridge.

- ▲ Ensure bench tops are not strewn with day-to-day junk.
- ▲ Make the beds and plump those cushions up.
- ▲ Open windows and blinds tidily.
- ▲ Mow the yard.

If you don't want to splash out on professional photos, do at least check your agent's pictures and discuss their order of appearance in any online listings. In particular, you should check that the agent has included the following:

- ▲ An external front shot of your home or unit block, either as the main picture or at least in the top five pictures in the online ad. If the external front shot is not included, buyers will be suspicious as to why it's been excluded.
- ▲ Photographs of all of the outside areas (front and back), including gardens, verandas, porches, pools and so on.
- ▲ Photographs of each living space, including the kitchen, bathrooms and the master bedroom (if it is appealing and decorated nicely).
- ▲ Photographs showing any structural features of the house, such as decorative windows, fireplaces or fittings.
- ▲ Shots of any impressive views.

The following should be avoided:

- ▲ Pointless photos of the kids' bedrooms, unless those rooms have any particular noteworthy feature.
- ▲ Misleading photos: fish-eye lenses that widen rooms artificially can result in the buying public expecting an enormous room when there is a far more humble space waiting for them on arrival. This tactic rarely works.

If you're not happy with the photographs your agent has put together, it's essential to let him or her know as soon as possible. I often hear sellers complaining about the pictures of their home that appear in advertisements, but when I enquire as to what the agent has done about it, I'm usually told that the seller hasn't even mentioned their concerns! If you're not satisfied with the agent's service, and you've been unable to negotiate a product that you're happy with, it may be worth considering hiring a professional photographer and paying separately for this service.

Choosing an agent

Choosing the right agent to sell your property is an important but difficult task. When choosing an agent, look for someone who is professional, knowledgeable about your area, willing to learn about your property and capable of estimating your property's value in a manner in which they can clearly justify. Most importantly, you should be able to work with him or her to get the sale over the line. Before you settle on an agent, do some research; meet a few local agents, and make sure your chosen agent adheres to the following criteria:

- The agent should have a good understanding of your locality, as well as the trends that characterise the local market.

- Ideally, he or she should have had success selling properties similar to yours. This isn't essential, but some background knowledge is vital.

- You must like the agent. You'll be working closely with your agent and you should expect regular contact even if there is nothing to report.

- The agent should have a good reputation. You can check this by asking for personal recommendations and to see any testimonials.

- Ensure you're comfortable with the agent's marketing style. Ask for examples of recent campaigns and check their write-ups and advertising style, both online and in print.

- Finally, consider the agency the agent belongs to. You should ensure your agent belongs to a good team in a well-located and well-run office. Is the office smart, in a good location and when visited were you greeted politely and helped efficiently? It is this office that will be representing your home so it is important.

What should you expect from an agent?

Once you have chosen your agent, you may be wondering what to expect. Remember that any agent appointed to sell your property is acting on *your* behalf, so that is how you should approach your relationship with him or her. Ask as many questions as you can about fees, terms and conditions, marketing campaigns, pictures and write-ups. Following is a list of legitimate expectations to have of your agent:

- All inspections and open homes should be followed up within 24 hours. The agent should provide you with feedback (good or bad) about the buyers' comments. You should be given notice of all inspections, and unless the home is vacant, notice to allow you to prepare, too.

- You should receive weekly updates about the progress the agent is making with selling your property, even if nothing has occurred. Expect to ascertain what kind of feedback buyers are giving about the home, the number of enquiries compared with other homes and the agent's interpretation of the feedback.

- The agent's colleagues should come to see your home too—this is called a 'caravan' and is vital, because it means other agents within the office know about your home and may know of a possible buyer.

- If a sale has not occurred after a couple of months, expect the agent to re-write your marketing campaigns and use new pictures of your property.

- Face-to-face meetings should be held between you and your agent if the house has not sold after two or three months.

- The agent should be monitoring *all* responses in relation to the pricing and appeal of your home, both good and bad, then reporting this information for you to stay informed just in case you want to consider a new marketing strategy or pricing adjustment.

- Expect backup from your agent's colleagues when your agent is sick or has a day off.

The secret property market

Just as there is a secret job market (where it is possible to get a job that hasn't been advertised), there is a secret property market. Only an agent can get you insight into these secret property markets.

Generally, the secret property market operates like this: before homes are listed for sale, agents will often know if someone is planning to move — not because they are psychic, but because they know who has approached them or their colleagues about the possibility of selling. Or maybe they have met certain parties interested in housing stock currently for sale but know that to facilitate this purchase they would have to sell an existing home which is currently not for sale. This kind of insider information is the real market knowledge that all other resources can only dream of.

Does this secret market help you as a seller? Well, sometimes it can by allowing a particularly active agent to inspect your home to let them know you may consider selling and if they knew anyone who would be possibly interested. It can be a little insight before you go to market, because if some interest is received, you could take this is a signal of possible high demand.

What agents should expect from you (yes, it does work both ways!)

In order to maximise the agent's success in selling your home, you should ensure the following are provided:

- Easy access to your home should be granted for inspections, even on short notice.

- A key to your property should be given to the agent in case he or she needs to show a client around your home when you're not around.

- A flexible attitude is expected of you as a seller. You need to listen to buyers' reactions to your property, and consider addressing issues if they seem to be stopping a sale.

- Good communication is expected from all sellers. Please let your agent know of changes in your circumstances as they arise.

- Try to always either be out or hidden in the garage during inspections. It is so off-putting for buyers to see the owners lurking around!

What if the agent doesn't perform?

Real estate is a people business, and if you and the agent are not getting on it is best to get out of the relationship early. Ditch the unsatisfactory agent as soon as you can. If you are really not working well together, he or she might allow you to walk away, even from an exclusive agreement.

If the agent doesn't perform, you should let him or her know — avoiding issues doesn't help anyone. Before you do complain, though, ensure that your grievance is fair and reasonable. Agents tend to get blamed even for things that are out of their control, and this will do nothing to help your relationship.

If the agent ignores your complaint, direct your concerns to the principal of the real estate company for which the agent works. If no action is taken after your complaint to the principal, your real estate institute should be the next port of call.

Discount fee or fixed fee agencies

In every state, a number of agencies operate on the basis of low standard commission fees or fixed fees, and therefore substantially undercut the normal prices charged by other agents.

Competition is good, of course, and these discounted services have been around since the '80s.

These agencies only currently form a very small part of any area's real estate services but they are an option available. There is only one benefit to the seller in dealing with agencies of this type and that is reduced costs, and in some cases those savings can be substantial.

Typically discounted agencies either operate on a fee of say just 1 per cent, or with a fixed fee schedule perhaps starting around $4000 or $5000. They usually have offices the same as the regular agencies and conduct their business exactly the same as agencies charging two or three times as much. I have one concern, though: traditional agencies across Australia are not necessarily raking it in. To attract the best sales people, remuneration is vital. Agents will get anything from 40 per cent to 60 per cent of the commission earned on a sale. That sounds like a lot, but they only ever get paid when a sale is agreed and settled. Based on conventional fees, a normal fee may be $10 000, so the sales person gets paid based on that. At the discount agent, the sales person may get a much lower percentage; the agent has to sell twice as many houses or expect half the normal salary. Based on these fees it is quite common for these agencies to be owner run and operated so the owner can retain 100 per cent of the low fee.

If in your area there is a discounted agency service, it may be worth including them in your list of agents to consider.

So the pros are clear: you have a great chance of saving money.

The cons include the agency not being able to recruit top agents, and a number of these companies tend to advertise their discounted fees on their listings for homes both online and in the print media so buyers will see you using a discounted service. This can sometimes encourage those buyers to calculate your possible saving and reduce it from their offer. Cheeky, but I have seen this happen!

Selling privately

A private sale is simply where a seller sells their home without an agent. Because no agent is involved the auction and tender method are not possible so the sale will be conducted using the private treaty method. A private sale is simply that—

a negotiation between the buyer and the seller and their res-pective lawyers.

Before you decide to go ahead with this option, it pays to first consider the reality of the situation you're getting yourself into. Yes, the option of saving thousands of dollars in agents' fees might seem attractive, but remember that as a private seller, you'll have to do all the work that the agent normally does on your own. This means taking responsibility for a number of tasks that the agent would usually take care of, including:

- preparing any paperwork you may need
- organising marketing and writing the copy for both the print and internet listings
- placing adverts and listings on websites available to private sellers
- receiving all phone call enquiries and answering emails
- organising or taking photographs
- conducting inspections and 'open houses'
- conducting all negotiations pre-sale
- dealing with queries that may be raised by the buyer's lawyer after a sale is agreed
- being available for buyers' organised inspections for valuers or building inspectors

Some people (mostly those who promote alternative selling services, I dare to say) claim that selling without the help of an agent is the way to go, but I haven't heard of many people doing so without at least some help from local agents in terms of clarifying sales prices or providing general advice. It may be that selling methods will evolve in the coming years to make private selling easier, but that matter is one for another book entirely.

If you do wish to soldier on through the complicated business of selling your home yourself, the following pages outline the main tasks you will need to be responsible for.

Prepare your paperwork

Paperwork is the dreaded element of any serious and grown-up undertaking, so before I scare you off, yes, you are trying to sell your home without an agent, but you are not trying to sell your home without a legal representative. Trying to sell your home without legal advice is absolutely not an option. Selling houses comes with huge volumes of paperwork and procedures as soon as you have an interested party who may want to buy. Before you begin any of the other preparatory work for selling your home, you *must* find yourself a legal representative.

If you decide to sell privately, ensure you have a sales contract prepared in advance. In some states you cannot market your home until a contract is ready, but no matter where you are located I strongly advise organising a contract first.

Your lawyer will be your guide when it comes to compiling your paperwork. What you need varies from state to state, and can include: details of your mortgage; copies of building warranties, if applicable; copies of warranties and guarantees on appliances; approval documents for any alterations you have made such as extensions; and drainage plans and approval for gas or electrical systems.

Plan your marketing campaign

There are numerous ways you can let prospective buyers know that your house is for sale as a private seller. You should take advantage of as many as possible to ensure you have the maximum amount of exposure. This will increase your chances of getting a high sale price.

Online listings

The internet is one option for marketing your home as a private seller. Without an agent, you will be responsible for compiling your listing, which means writing your advertising copy, taking photos and submitting your ad to your chosen websites. Be aware that the website <www.realestate.com.au> doesn't allow private sellers because their revenue is generated from selling their space to agents.

Another option is to list your home on a private seller's website, but unfortunately these are not nearly as popular in the mass market as <www.domain.com.au> and <www.realestate.com. au>, so there is the potential you may not successfully reach your chosen market.

Print media

The local property supplements and house-selling magazines are usually available to all types of sellers, so you can advertise your home along with all the agents' listings. If you live in the area you are selling in you will know the most popular papers for property advertising and the days on which the property sections appear. Most suburbs also have property listing magazines that are printed monthly or fortnightly. If you are not sure which ones are popular, go past your local real estate agent as they often have all the local free property magazines and property supplements outside their offices. If you are not in the area, go online and search local newspapers for that town.

If you choose to advertise in these supplements, you'll need to do the following things:

- Write advertising copy and include the suburb, price, contact details and a basic accommodation list plus a catchy heading. Avoid too much text and use bullet points to highlight the features.

- Take photos. Ask the publication (or check on their website) what quality and file size they need for their photos. If you only have one picture ensure it is the best you can get. Ideally an exterior front shot is preferable but if your home has a view, a great pool or a fantastic garden, you can use these, too.

- Give an email address and maybe a link to a website where potential buyers can see more.

'For sale' boards

Having a 'for sale' board in front of your house is a great source of advertising, but get a professional company to create one; hand written on an old piece of board is just not the look! A successful board must:

- look professional

- state 'for sale' with your contact details and an email address or link to a website where the home is listed

- have minimal text in addition to the contact details—I suggest no more than a catchy heading such as 'luxury living' or 'the family dream' and a few bullet points including number of bedrooms, house size and block size

- not state the price, as this is rarely disclosed on boards

- include a picture of the interior or the backyard (ensure the quality is suitable to be enlarged)—do not include the front of the house, as they can already see it!

Local sign makers are your best bet for board making. Otherwise, look up printing companies in the *Yellow Pages*.

Conduct inspections

Conducting open inspections can be one of the trickiest tasks for private sellers. There are two different types of inspections: the 'by appointment' type and an 'open house'. Inspections should follow these guidelines:

- Ensure there's an order to the way in which you show the home: always start with accommodation inside, then outside areas.

- Keep the inspection moving. Never dwell too long in each room—once all the areas are covered, enquire as to whether the buyer would like to have another look around. On the second round, give them space to wander more freely (within reason—always be aware of the possible security risk of letting a stranger loose in your home!). When they've completed the second round, the backyard is a great place to leave them for a chat with their partner or family—not much to pinch out there!

- Ascertain the buyer's knowledge of your suburb. If he or she is not familiar with the available facilities, amenities and travel distances between places, help out by being as informative as possible.

- Try to keep conversations with buyers flowing smoothly. Enquire as to the buyer's circumstances, and find out what they're looking for.

- Once the inspection is complete, ask the prospective buyers if they have any questions. Allow them to leave without harrassing them—if they want to buy, leaving after the inspection without making an offer will not stop them.

- Do not over sell. For example, avoid such comments as 'we have had *loads* of interest', or 'it's a high-demand area, so we expect to sell quickly', or even 'everyone *loves* our home'. All these phrases just make you sound desperate. Stick with facts, and let the home sell itself. If you have lived in the home for a good length of time (say, five years or more), make sure potential buyers know this, because that indicates it has been a good home for you.

So keep that inspection moving, stick to polite general chat, don't push the buyer but ask general questions about their search. Of course, if everyone reads this book (I can wish!) we'll have to change strategy soon enough!

Negotiations

If you think inspections are tricky, you'll struggle with negotiations. This is where the *real* hard work begins, and is also where a private seller can lose out substantially. The reason sellers initiate the private sale option is to save money, but some savvy buyers will use the fact that you are saving on agents' fees to reduce their offer accordingly, so all your work will have been in vain. You are going to have to be pretty tough to avoid offers that are too low, and you may never know whether you have succeeded or not. It is also difficult as a private seller to undertake background checks on prospective buyers, because their lawyer is unlikely to speak to you directly because you are not a client of theirs, or a licensed agent, whereas agents often speak to a buyer's lawyers for clarification and updates.

To succeed, you need to be very confident on your target sales figure. You should be realistic, while still trying to push the potential buyer as far as you can, but stopping before they walk away. This is without doubt the most awkward part of a private sale, for both the seller *and* the buyer, so please be warned: if you are a natural-born negotiator, you may well succeed; but most of you will probably struggle.

Remember, by definition, 'negotiation' is a comp-romise between buyer and seller. If you react to an offer with a 'barrier' response and display no give-and-take, a buyer might feel compromised, and some will not buy privately for this very reason.

Other selling services

Until very recently, you either sold your home privately or employed an agent. But in the past few years, a whole new breed of internet-based services have sprung up in the marketplace. This is such a new phenomenon that it is still early days for these services, so looking at their long-term history isn't possible.

When online services began they tended to be a way a private seller could list their home for sale. This service alone was hardly enough because unless buyers know to search that particular website, they will never see your home so you would still have to do all the work of a private sale too. So unless that website is attracting a vast amount of buyer traffic, it is unlikely to reach sufficient buyers to make it an attractive option for sellers.

As online services have progressed a variety of innovative services have become available. One example is vendor advocacy. In this case, a company acts as your advocate and guides you through the selling process by advising you on everything from your home presentation to selecting an agent, and holds your hand every step of the way.

The plus side of vendor advocacy is the attentive service you will receive. That said, I have spoken to a number of agents who have refused to participate in vendor advocacy (the agent must agree to split his or her fee with the advocate) as they don't believe it offers any benefit to the seller other than adding another party into the mix. So buyer beware!

If you are interested in finding out more, see <www.ldb.com.au> (Victoria), <www.propertybuyer.com.au> (New South Wales) or <www.vendoradvocacy.com.au> (Australia wide).

Another new contender in the online world is <www.buy myplace.com.au>. This company will list your home, order boards, have your home valued, have a representative conduct inspections for you, undertake marketing, organise photographs, conduct open inspections and even deal with all enquiries and negotiations—they will even take your home to auction! Costs start from as little as $250.

Which option is for me?

In order to compare the three main selling techniques you need to consider that 'added expenses' are applicable and unavoidable with all options. Pictorial 'for sale' boards, professional photographs, floor plans, title searches, legal expenses, internet advertising and print advertising are all costs no matter how you sell.

The real comparable is the agency fee. A traditional agency will charge you anything from 2 to 3 per cent plus GST of the value of your home. For a $500 000 home that is between $11 000 and $16 500 including GST.

Generally, a discounted agency service could equate to around $5500 to $6600 including GST on the same home. If you are paying for a full service, you will have to do very little other than go out for inspections and be available to talk to the agent when required.

Online services cost from $200 to $2500 depending on what that service is offering you, but you will have to be more involved in the whole process.

Private selling obviously costs nothing over and above the 'expenses', but you have to handle the whole lot with no help.

In conclusion, as this book is about the truth not the flannel, I'll make it simple for you: personally, I would still use an agent to sell my home, but alternatives are out there. These options could become far more prominent over the next few years, so watch this space. It could be that the whole world of real estate as we know it changes substantially. Only time will tell.

. . . .

What's the agent thinking?

Once agents spot your private ad or board—well, let's say it is like a red rag to a bull.

Firstly, the agent is thinking that you should use his or her services, and that you'd be mad to try any other option! In fact, he or she is thinking that you'll end up with an agent anyway. (This is actually pretty likely because the majority of property transactions in Australia are handled by real estate agents.)

The agent will be rather annoyed if you enlisted their services at the start but never followed through with the deal and ended up selling privately. They may have helped you by suggesting market values, things to make the home better for sale and so on—only for you to waste their time and try to sell privately.

At this point, they would not only like to send you an invoice for their time, but they will also deeply hope that you fail to sell. They might even consider ringing the local pizza delivery company for unsolicited late-night pizza deliveries twice a week for a month!

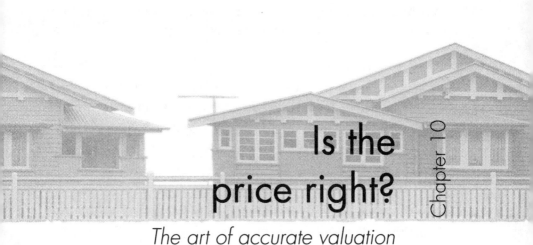

Is the price right?

The art of accurate valuation

The most pressing question homeowners ask in the lead-up to selling their property is: 'What is my home worth?'

Now, as surprising as this may seem, there is actually a simple and definitive answer to this question. Yes, I can actually tell you your home's exact value—without even knowing anything about it. Your house is worth ...

Wait for it ...

... *exactly the amount that a buyer is prepared to pay for it.*

Most people believe that their home is worth the sum they *want* to achieve when they sell. This belief is often formed by following a train of thought such as this: when comparing their home with other homes, the seller had noted that their place is *much* better than the others are. Also, they've invested *at least* $60 000 worth of time and energy in building a deck out the back, and since they bought the house more than seven years ago, it *must* have doubled in value since they purchased it, right?

Wrong!

No matter how much you want your home to achieve a certain price, remember that you do not have the ultimate control. The buyer chooses the offer they make, and at what point they increase their offer or walk away—it is all up to them.

Sellers often cling to the myth that their fantasy sale price is viable because 'someone out there' will surely pay the inflated price they've conjured up. When I hear such things, I always want to ask the seller where, exactly, 'out there' is. If you are a seller who actually manages to find the elusive 'out there'—where the buyers are cashed up, clueless and completely naive about the housing market—please let me know! I will move there and set up shop.

 I can recall numerous occasions where misguided sellers have blown their chances of achieving a high sale price, or have ended up with less than their original estimated value, because they *believed they knew better than the buyer did*. Don't be the next victim!

I know of a mansion that recently sold at auction for $3.5 million —pretty good, eh? Well, it's not so good when you consider that the sellers received an offer of $4.5 million prior to auction, but refused to accept it 'just in case' they could get more at auction. This is a classic example of a seller failing to understand that a house is worth as much as someone will pay for it, *not* what you think it will sell for. If I had a dollar for every time I have heard a seller comment that they 'wished they had taken a buyer's initial offer', or that they are 'just holding out until a buyer will pay their desired price'—well, I would have been able afford the mansion I just mentioned.

Of course, the seller does have some role to play. As a seller, you can choose how much to list your house for. You can choose to accept or decline offers made by prospective buyers. But how do you know what is unrealistic? How do you know when to draw the line? For starters, you need to research the current market, be brutally honest about where your home sits in the market, and understand that buyers have the final say.

Testing the market

Testing the market is an option that sellers often take if they believe that, despite all the information and advice they have probably received from valuers and agents, there is still a buyer out there willing to pay more. It is where a seller lists their home for an inflated price, just to see whether or not it will sell.

This practice is loved by sellers, but loathed by most agents and buyers. The price the seller expects to get when testing the market is always above market value, and certainly higher than the price that those 'clueless local agents' suggested — because why would *they* know anything? They only sell homes in your area day in and day out — the fools!

Testing the market doesn't actually help anyone, not even the seller, because the house will only ever sell if the asking price is viable. All testing the market does is distort the *actual* market, by adding to stock levels and encouraging other sellers to list their properties at inflated prices that match the inaccurate, exaggerated prices of the testers. Alternatively, testing the market can make sensibly priced homes seem like great value, further decreasing the tester's chance of a sale.

Testing the market annoys genuine buyers and good agents. As for the agents that allow these testers to hit the market with madly inflated prices, well, they need a telling off. Listen here, agents: you won't sell a house if its listed price is too far above market value — you will just waste your time and money listing it. Then, when the seller does decide to get real about the pricing, you will have failed in your client's eyes. They will simply instruct a new agent at a new price — so stop encouraging sellers to test the market!

To be able to start any pricing research you need to have a rough idea of what a home like yours may sell for. A rough estimate could be based on what you paid plus how much you think the value may have risen, or perhaps you know a home similar to yours sold last year—a rough guide is all you need to get started. (Or you can stop reading right now and hire a professional property valuer to do all the work for you. There's absolutely nothing wrong with that!)

Establishing a correct selling price

The 'correct' selling price of a property is what you can convince a buyer to pay. This price will depend on a large number of variables, including:

- *Location.* Obviously, sellers whose homes are in high-demand locations can expect a higher selling price. A location can be in high demand for countless reasons, including the following: it is in a desirable school catchment; it has water or park views; the street is quiet (in busy suburbs); there is plentiful parking (in city locations) or easy access to public transport. The trick is to make sure you are comparing like with like. If a home has sold in the less desirable part of your suburb, the likelihood is that your home will sell for more, but you really should be comparing with a home that has very similar location advantages.

- *Specifications.* Certain features can attract more buyer interest and higher sale prices. Homes with potential often get higher sale figures than their similar neighbours; for example, corner homes often have possibilities for extension, subdivision or provision of extra parking space, even though the block size might be similar to others on the street. Homes presented in a contemporary style will get buyers excited whereas the one decorated and fitted in a more traditional style may not attract as much interest. Every suburb will have buyers with different specifications on their wishlists. The more you give a buyer what they want, the higher your price could be.

- *Age and condition.* The age and condition of a property impacts heavily on the price a seller can expect. With any home, the condition of the property is where you have total control — the interior and exterior are equally as important. Older homes are only ever desirable when they have character and a certain style. Most housing built before the 1950s has a chance of being desirable in any condition because unmodernised, it is a renovator's dream and modernised, it is a charming unique home. From the 1950s onwards, homes lost some of their character, and as such unrenovated homes from this era on require a major facelift to get a top selling price. This is where you have to be honest with yourself. If your kitchen or bathroom are more than 10 years old, you may have to review your price expectations or do some upgrades.

- *Market conditions.* Whether a home is being sold in a buyers' market or a sellers' market will dictate the price a buyer is willing to pay. For an explanation of buyers' and sellers' markets, see pages 18 and 19.

- *Marketing.* A seller or agent who is very skilled at marketing and who provides maximum positive exposure to a property can increase the amount that can be expected. For more on marketing, refer to chapter 9.

- *Presentation.* The way the home is presented at open inspections and in marketing material can affect the amount of buyer interest, and therefore the price. For more information on home staging, see chapter 9.

- *Method of sale.* The way a house is sold can often play a part in the ultimate sale figure obtained. For further information, see chapter 11.

When determining how these factors will impact on your sale price, there are several things you can do to ensure your proposed sale price is accurate and viable. These include:

- conducting your own online research about recent sales

- checking out the competition by inspecting homes similar to yours that are for sale

- going to open inspections to see for yourself what you're up against

- comparing your home to the competition (while being brutally honest with yourself)

- analysing the market

- enlisting the assistance of several agents to provide you with a professional estimate of price.

Each of these things will be discussed in detail on the following pages.

Andrew's hot tip

Think back to when you bought the property originally, and ask yourself the following questions: How did your sale price stack up next to the competition back then? What was the price difference between properties that had more bedrooms, or better views than yours?

Researching recent sales figures

When attempting to estimate the market value of your home, your first port of call should always be online research. As mentioned in chapter 2, the best websites to use when finding out past sale prices are <www.rpdata.com>, <www.pdslive.com.au> and <www.residex.com.au>.

These sites charge for accessing details, but it can be worth the fee to ensure your knowledge is accurate and up to date. They often provide extensive details about recently sold homes, including:

- the sale price

- the home's block size

- an aerial view
- the number and type of rooms
- photographs
- median values in the area
- population growth in the area
- suburb history.

The amount of information provided on the site will depend on the specific property and on the website itself. Ideally, you should research houses similar to yours and compare their features and prices to the features your home has. Because no two suburbs are the same, information about sale prices obtained in your area will give you the best idea of what your home might be worth. If your house has features that are very rare in your own area, you may want to research similar properties in nearby suburbs. This will help you work out how much value a particular feature adds to the price of the home. Be realistic, though—if the suburb you are researching has sea views and huge block sizes while yours doesn't, concentrate your research on a suburb that has more features similar to yours.

Researching the competition

Having ascertained the recent history of sale prices for homes similar to yours, you should check out the competition by researching homes that are currently for sale. The features and expected price ranges of these immediate 'competition houses' will be more up to date than the ones you researched when investigating historic sales figures. Some useful websites that list properties for sale are: <www.domain.com.au> and <www. realestate.com.au>.

In order to make a realistic comparison between your home and the competition, it might be helpful to ascertain what the median price of the properties that you have researched is. The median price is the middle figure of all the homes in your search category. This information is also available on the websites

<www.domain.com.au> and <www.realestate.com.au>, if you search under suburb information.

Now that you have the median figure for your search band and suburb, you know where your desired asking price will sit in relation to the other houses in the area. In order to illustrate how this could help you to narrow down your competition, let's say you think your home is worth $500000 and your suburb median is $400000, and the highest recorded sale in the last year in your suburb was $800000. In this case, I would suggest comparing your home with the houses in the search range of $400000 to $600000 in your suburb and those close by.

As you do this I want you to imagine the nightmare of me looking over your shoulder as you smile and claim that your kitchen and garden are far better than the houses you're looking at. Are you sure I wouldn't be tapping you on your shoulder and asking you to really be honest about your home? We all have a tendency to think our homes are better than everyone else's, when in fact those tough, demanding and ever-so-critical buyers may not. Just keep that thought of my menacing presence hanging over your shoulder and you should avoid mistakes!

(Please note that this pricing exercise is to be used as a guide and is part of all the other research and information you gather. The trick is applying all this knowledge to your home without bias, and that is not easy; after all, it's your home and you have an emotional connection to it.)

Cast your net wide

It's important to look at a wide range of properties if you want to gain a realistic view of the market. If you estimate your property to be valued under $500000, also consider those priced $50000 under and over your target when looking at the competition. If you expect your property to sell for $500000 or more, expand that net to $100000 under and over. I know this sounds like a wide range, but it will really give you an insight into the market.

Similarly, if you have a one-bedroom unit, look at one- and two-bedroom units to see what you are up against. If you have a four-bedroom freestanding home, you could search for five-bedroom homes as well.

When looking at the competition, it's important to keep the following things in mind:

- *Street quality.* Consider the quality of the street (by using Google's Street View feature, or visiting the location in person), so you can realistically compare it with yours. Be honest with yourself about whether the homes listed are in better or poorer locations than yours.

- *Size and features of block and outdoor areas.* Keep your block size in mind while you're searching. A large block could add significant value. The availability of onsite parking and the size of any outdoor entertaining areas is also important. This has a wide percentage variant as each buyer has their own needs regarding outdoor space. Also, smaller outdoor spaces can have a different effect on value depending on house type. For example, a smaller-than-average garden might not affect the value of a townhouse as much as it would a family home. Blocks that are very hilly can also limit the value add of a larger outdoor space.

- *Age and design style of property.* Age has a negative impact by different degrees: if the home is ugly and dated it is at the higher deduction end of the scale, old but with charm is not too bad and not quite so old but with a good design is okay. This is a hard one because you have to try to judge your home's beauty compared with others in the area, and make a realistic comparison. My first home was as architecturally stimulating as a 1970s office building, but did it have a negative effect on its value? Not really, because most of the homes in the area were like that!

- *Proximity to main roads.* If your home is on a main road, its value will often be reduced compared to other homes in the area because of noise and aspect. The worst scenario is the main road position in a normally quiet suburb, which could mean a percentage drop of as much as 15 to 20 per cent. Another home set back from the main road in a nice suburb would drop by only 10 to 15 per cent. In a quiet rural area a home on a main road could drop by as much as 20 to 30 per cent. An inner-city main road location would not impact as severely as the others and only have a percentage drop of no more than 10 per cent. Likewise if your home is in a quiet street compared with other properties in your area, you can calculate the value increase by adding these above percentages.

- *Availability of views.* A view of a park, any waterway or across an attractive landscape will add substantial value to your home, so be aware of this when checking out the competition.

- *Proximity to facilities.* If your home is within walking distance of a great school, you could see an increase in value of around 1 to 3 per cent as opposed to an identical home that is nearby but not within walking distance. A similar situation exists for transport: a home within walking distance will probably be valued at between 1 and 5 per cent higher than an identical home that is just a little further away. And the beach is a big one: a home within 500 metres of the beach is likely to be valued between 5 and 15 per cent higher than an identical place just 1 kilometre away. Definite food for thought!

- *Quality of floor plan.* A poorly thought out floor plan can have a big impact on the value of a home. If you (or houses you are comparing yours with) have a separate kitchen away from living areas, an exterior laundry or a bathroom or toilet that is not near your bedroom, chances are your value will be affected—often by as much as a whopping 20 per cent! Also keep an eye on your room balance; if this is out of whack, your value might suffer. For example, do you have a spacious home but a tiny kitchen? Or a huge master bedroom but very small secondary bedrooms? If so, take this into consideration. Restructuring a floor plan is expensive and complicated, which is why a bad floor plan can have such an enormous effect on value.

Be brutally honest about your home

You have to be really brutal in your evaluation of your home's value. You may recently have spent $30 000 on getting a new kitchen and pool installed, but if you went for the blue doors and the wildly patterned tiles, you might not get as much bang for your buck as you think. Similarly, you may have installed a pool, but because you used up the whole backyard to fit it, there's no space for children to play in the winter months. The value added by this $30 000 in improvements may be negligible to some prospective buyers, because they will want to rip the whole thing out and replace it with a new kitchen that better suits their tastes, or take the pool out to create garden space.

Attending open inspections

People who attend open inspections with no intention of buying are agents' nightmares, but in this chapter I have my 'researcher' hat on; if you want to know what's out there in the market, there's nothing wrong with going and having a little sticky beak.

Although websites can give you very good information about the homes your property is competing with, attending open inspections or watching nearby auctions is infinitely more helpful in terms of working out what you're up against. This is because every home is different, and websites do not necessarily give details about the presentation of the home, the quality of the kitchen and bathroom fittings, whether the previous owners just had good old-fashioned bad taste, or even if the floor plan works.

Inspections can give you a direct comparison between your home and similar homes on the market. You might even learn some tips for presenting your home in the best possible way!

Analysing current market conditions

Having researched the recent sale prices for properties similar to yours and checked out the current competition, you need to get a good idea of what the current property market looks like. From the perspective of a seller, the key question you should be asking is, 'How strong is the current demand for a product such as mine?' How well the demand is being met by the availability (or supply) of properties similar to yours also comes into it; even the best home at the best price will never sell unless there is demand for it. Becoming familiar with the level of demand for a certain house type at a specific time will tell you whether you can push your price expectations up or whether you'll need to lower your expectations. You should gather most of this information on properties based locally, but to gain a bigger picture, you should look at the property market generally, too.

Putting your ideas to the test

You will know if your proposed sale figure is viable within two or three months of putting the house on the market. Assuming that you have marketed the house skilfully, if your target price has not been met within three months, your price is too high. If this happens, you should either adjust your expectations and lower your price, or postpone your sale until the market shows some improvement. If you choose the latter option, remember that your target figure may well eventually be achieved — but the homes you are looking to buy will also most likely have increased in price. So you may gain nothing from all that waiting!

There are a few things you can do to learn about the current property market:

📠 Read media stories, but be aware that they are often sensationalised or misleading. Newspapers and online sites such as <www.businessday.com.au> and <www.apimagazine.com.au> are good sources of information.

📠 Remember that what you are trying to establish with your research is a current housing market pattern and whether it will have a positive or negative impact on your area and your type of home, so only take note of reports in the last three months.

📠 Try to gauge whether the subject being reported on will actually affect your forthcoming sale. For example, a 'first home purchasers leaving the market' headline may affect your home if it is in the area's first homebuyers' price range, but if you are further up the ladder, the slowdown in that sector may not filter through to your price range for several months, so you should try to sell quickly. Even stock market reports publishing bad results can lead to more buyers and investors in the housing market because they want to put their money into a safer investment rather than the volatile stock market.

Getting the agents in

Having completed your own research about the competition and the state of the property market, you are ready to enlist the help of your local agents. No-one else in the property market has a more direct link to the housing market than the local agents. Agents are continually contacted by the buying public,

221

so they have a very up-to-date and well-informed picture of the housing market.

Beware the ceiling price

Every locality will have a ceiling price: the maximum amount buyers will spend on a property in your street before they can find a similar property for the same price in a better street or area. This concept is particularly relevant to estimating sale price if your home is already at the top of its market (that is, it's one of the better houses in the street or area). In these cases, you can't count on getting a higher sale price for your property because of improvements that you've made, or special features that your home has. For this reason, when you are making improvements to your home for the purpose of selling, you need to be aware that the value of your home won't necessarily reflect the amount you've spent on improvements.

So how does this concept translate into practice? Well, if your home's value is already at the high end of the market in your area (because it's larger than the others are, or the block or view is better), there's no point in getting carried away with luxuries such as adding a pool, doing up the kitchen or adding an extra bedroom. Your home is already at its ceiling price. A buyer won't spend, for example, $1 million on your home if they can get a similar product for the same money in a better street — *no matter how many improvements you've made.* If you do need to improve a bit to sell, expect increased saleability as opposed to a definite value gain.

In order to get a rough idea of what the ceiling price might be in your street or suburb, search online listings for the highest prices, or consult the reports on sites such as <www.rpdata.com>, <www.pdslive.com.au> or <www.residex.com.au>. Usually for detailed suburb reports you will have to pay a fee, but it is worthwhile doing so because not only will it help you ascertain the ceiling price, it will break down the market prices, too.

So are these agent folk incredibly talented university types with more brain cells than Stephen Hawking (or at least an understanding of valuation principles that goes beyond the average Bruce or Sheila's comprehension)? Sadly, no. However, I will divulge the secret of why agents know their stuff: their knowledge is current and comprehensive. It's as simple as that. They know what is selling in their own agency, and they make sure they know what their competitors are selling for.

The reason you should do your own research *before* you talk to an agent is to ensure that you can pick the clueless ones, the desperate ones, the ones who will list your property at an inflated price hoping to beat you down later or the ones that list low and sell to their friends and relatives — it does happen. (For more on dubious valuations, see chapter 10.)

I am pleased to say that the dodgy, the darn-right-devious and the cunning-like-sharks agents are in the minority, and if you have done your research, you will be able to spot their games or mistakes early on in the process.

How does the agent deliver 'that' figure?

Contrary to popular belief, not all agents are the same. (Honestly!) Each individual will have his or her own unique way of arriving at 'that' figure. In a booming market, it is a pure pleasure to tell clients that they will make more money than they thought; it's rather unpleasant delivering the awful news that the value of the client's home has plummeted since they last had it valued. Agents all have their own style, but they generally fall into three broad categories (I bet you can recognise these if you have had the pleasure of dealing with agents!).

Mr or Ms Useless: the Mr and Ms Useless of the real estate world are easy to spot. They often arrive at your home unprepared and 20 minutes late, having been lost on the way to your home because they don't know your street. When asked, they tell you that they can't be sure what has sold recently in your suburb (in fact, they didn't even know that next door was up for sale!). They get a bit nervous when you ask for an estimate on the spot — and this is particularly surprising because your home is of a common size and specification in your area, and you've been told that your home is easy to value.

Mr or Ms Useless might be a very nice person, and should be given the benefit of the doubt (they may be new to your area or new to the agency). But really, no agent should arrive unprepared or without a colleague to hold their hand if they're unsure of their abilities.

The price estimates given by Mr or Ms Useless could be anything from nearly believable to way off the mark. The figure may or may not tie in with your research and, to be frank, *you* may be more on the mark than *they* are. So whatever they say, be nice, say thanks and wait for the next agent.

Mr or Ms Clued Up: you can spot clued-up agents a mile away. They arrive on time; they know your house, your street and your suburb better than you do; they remember every single recent sale and every feature of the area. They can speak with authority about your home's features and presentation as it relates to current buyers' demand. They may even comment that they know someone who could be interested (this may be a sweetener or an exaggeration, but if they are this clued up, they possibly *do* know someone!). Listen to their figures, and listen to their reasons for having arrived at the figures.

Mr or Ms 'I Want That Listing No Matter What': how can you tell if you're dealing with an agent who only cares about securing your listing, no matter what they have to tell you in order to get it? Well, the first thing they'll do is flatter you with an unrealistically high price in order to get you excited about working with them. Be aware that they are only doing this because they intend to slowly wear you down, and sell your home for a regular sum in the end. There is nothing more flattering than an agent being excited about your home—in fact, it is essential. But too much hype at the start of the process can end in disappointment. It is very easy to fall under their spell, so, watch out!

In a very good market, quite a few agents will surprise you in a positive way—but always get them to justify their figures. A clued-up agent will have no problems explaining the logic behind his or her valuation, but a clueless agent, or an agent who just wants a listing, will start to sweat. He or she will avoid the question at all costs, often by being unnaturally nice to you, commenting on your lovely perm or mullet, your dog, or (even more worrying) being nice to your kids!

This type of agent will not be able to sell your house for the original price quoted to you. They will try to convince you to drop the price after a while, claiming the market is quiet or prices seem to be going down. Alternatively, they'll let your property pass in at auction, or simply spend months trying (and failing) to sell it at the original unrealistic price. Eventually, you'll end up selling for less than if you had started at the right figure in the first place.

In my view, no good agent should ever agree to market a home for a figure that is unrealistic, but not all agents follow that policy.

Deciphering divergent values

Once you have sussed out the bad agents from the good, you have yet another problem: agents' estimates can vary. This is because valuation is an art rather than a science. Even experienced and knowledgeable agents will give you varying figures, so expect some deviations (within reason). For homes under $1 million, anything from 0 to 10 per cent variation is common. If the home is worth more than $1 million, the range of estimates can fluctuate 10 or 15 per cent—even more, sometimes.

If you have done your own research, you will always be in control, and won't be surprised that figures can go up and down in short periods of time. Always remember that your home is only worth what someone is prepared to pay for it.

How easy is it to value your home?

Your property will fit into one of just two categories when it comes to estimating a value. The technical terms for these categories are:

- 🏠 the easy ones to value
- 🏠 the bloody hard ones to value.

Houses are easier to value if the specifications, size and style are common in your area. In cases such as this, a fairly direct comparison can be made between properties that have sold recently or are currently for sale, and the property you are selling. It's fair to assume that if there's clearly a demand for the type of home you're selling in your area that your home could meet the expectations of the prospective buyers.

As I have stressed in other chapters, presentation can have a huge impact on the sale price you end up obtaining. A dedicated effort to ensure the house is looking fabulous on inspection days and in photographs can significantly boost the sale price.

In contrast, the bloody hard homes to value break the mould for an area. They may be much smaller or much bigger than the other houses, or their specifications might be completely different (in either a positive or a negative way). These are the homes that are just plain different—even just in terms of design or architectural style. Unique or unusual homes will be much more complicated to value, because you won't necessarily have anything to compare them to. So if you've employed an agent to value your home and he or she requests breathing space to think about an appropriate price for your 'bloody hard' home, give him or her a chance to think on it for a few days.

Negotiating on price

Now hold onto your hats—I'm about to give you some really amazing advice: you know how you want to sell your home for top dollar? Well, guess what? Buyers want to spend as little as possible! That's right, you read it here first.

The conflict between buyers and sellers is a fundamental issue when selling your home, so the way you deal with an offer depends on your understanding of the market and your knowledge of the buyer. This is very obvious if you are face to face negotiating in a private sale scenario with no agents, but it can be just as relevant when you have the benefit of an agent negotiating for you. The negotiations are the tricky part of the sale process, and even with an agent on board you need to know the market because your ability to think as the buyer will help you make sensible descisions. The key is to be armed with research to give you a position of strength, and if you know the market is flooded with homes like yours at similar prices you will know not to hang out for a top figure because buyers will just go elsewhere!

Your understanding of the market should come from your own research and agents' opinions. If all the advice you've received and the information you've researched is initially conflicting, it may be worthwhile paying for an independent valuer to put your mind at ease. By the time you start receiving offers, you should already have a realistic idea of what price to expect. Without this you will be unprepared for the negotiating process. In most cases the agent conducts the negotiation but ultimately you control it.

Following are some ideas about how to handle the negotiation process.

Don'ts:

- Don't get too personal. Some classic lines I hear from sellers receiving low offers include 'They are taking the mickey!'; 'They can take their offer and shove it—I wouldn't sell to them if they were the last buyers on Earth!'; or, 'These buyers are mad if they think we are that stupid!' A low offer is always frustrating, but before you get too critical, you should ask yourself if *you* have ever submitted a low offer. I bet you have! By getting personal, you will get all upset; you will end up getting even more bitter and twisted. So, ignore the personal factor—this is all about getting a deal.

- Don't be unrealistic. Although a certain figure may have been possible at the beginning of the marketing campaign, prices do go down. Don't blame buyers for this—when prices increase you don't get cross, do you? Also remember that the longer a home is listed on the market the lower its perceived value will be, as that length of time promotes the fact that interest in the property is low.

227

⌂ Don't dismiss offers without any thought. If a buyer submits a bid that is lower than expectations, ask them or your agent why—it is a perfectly reasonable question. Admittedly, some buyers will just be trying a low offer because they are more interested in a low price; after all, who isn't? But they could also be reducing their offer for a valid reason. Some legitimate reasons for a reduced offer include:

- ▢ the home may have been on the market for a long period of time, which advertises a lack of interest and could give buyers the impression they have the liberty to try low offers

- ▢ the home requires essential repairs and is not priced to allow for these

- ▢ market conditions have changed and sales have been lower recently.

Dos:

⌂ Do be aware that if a number of buyers are offering lower figures, the amounts they are offering are probably closer to the real value.

⌂ Do accept any structural or urgent improvements costs as a reasonable excuse to reduce an offer. Alternatively, be prepared to undertake the works yourself to obtain a higher figure.

⌂ Do negotiate! This will always be necessary unless a market is booming at the top of its cycle. You will know if the market is booming by the level of interest you are receiving.

When should you refuse an offer?

There are several legitimate reasons for refusing an offer:

⌂ If the buyers are not genuine, you should refuse the offer. But how will you know if they are not? You need to be able to prove that the buyers are prepared to make some financial commitment. If you discover that the buyers are offering on numerous properties, haven't checked out their finances or haven't even put their existing house on the market (unless they are purchasing your home for investment purposes, of course), then you might as well forget them.

- If you are confident (and have done extensive research to suggest) that the offer is clearly too low, you should refuse it. You'll know that the price offered is below market value if the agents' estimates confirm your own conclusions.

- If you believe that with a bit of negotiation a rejected initial offer can lead to a higher offer from the same party, you should consider refusing the offer. Look for signs of the buyer's level of interest. Are they able to buy with finances ready to go? Was their offer submitted soon after inspection? Do they seem to know what they want?

- If the terms of the proposed contract are unrealistic or just plain daft, you should refuse the offer. For example, if someone offers you a sensible (or even attractive) financial figure, but the contract is riddled with ridiculous conditions that are just not worth the paper they are written on, don't sign anything. For example, the sale may be dependent on the buyer selling their home; the contract may contain bizarre finance conditions wanting unusually extended periods of time; or the settlement dates may only suit the buyer. The terms of an offer are a huge element of this process, and you should only be flexible with terms and conditions if the market is slow.

The true value of an offer

Sellers always seem to focus on the sale figure, but when negotiating, you *must* take into account the other, non-fiscal, benefits you receive from the sale. This 'unquantifiable' value has implications for your lifestyle and peace, and can be particularly important for people who are selling to relieve mortgage stress or to allow them to get on with life without financial worries.

Some non-fiscal elements that should be considered are: the chance to move on with life by clearing debts, downsizing, releasing equity for holidays and hobbies or enabling the move to the bigger house that has enough room for all the family.

You can never exclude the value of these non-fiscal elements, especially in poor market conditions. Stubbornly refusing to sell because of a pre-existing expectation that you'd get a specific price can affect you and your family. Of course everyone wants the best price, but if market conditions are not allowing this and you have tried selling for a long period of time, you have to be brave and consider selling for a lower figure than you had planned. Hanging on for another few thousand (or, in some cases, even $50 000) might not be worth it, if peace of mind and physical and mental health are becoming problematic due to the ongoing sales stress. And remember that if you also repurchase in these same market conditions, it may be you make a good profit on the next home.

Financial benefits of selling

Selling immediately rather than drawing out the process could also have a number of financial benefits, because keeping your home on the market for too long involves several costs (which are often hidden). These may include:

- ongoing maintenance
- added expenses caused by the need to rent somewhere
- ongoing marketing costs
- costs of holding two properties (if you have already purchased another home), including extra mortgage costs.

I hope this chapter has given you an understanding of the many variables involved in valuing a home. The better equipped you are with your knowledge, the more likely you'll be to secure the best price possible for your home.

What's the agent thinking?

Picture this scene: Wayne and Noelene have shown the agent their beautifully presented home—their pride and joy. The agent knows that others have been in to make an estimate. So, what figure is the agent going to say? He or she will be aware that the announcement of the estimated value will be met by one of three possible responses: a delighted, smiley reaction; a quiet 'as we expected' look; or a look of complete horror followed by the comment: 'You must be mad! We wouldn't sell this place for that!'

Agents are generally nervous about putting a numerical value on your property. Even if they're good at their job and are confident, the act of stating a value will involve at least a little adrenaline rush, because the agent will automatically assume that the seller will have an unrealistically high figure in mind.

Unfortunately, many sellers have not read this book yet and the agents know this. Sellers always overvalue their own home, and it is not just private sellers, either—you bloody developers are mad too, and that's why you have to spend so much on creative marketing to justify those figures!

Surely, the most important thing should be that your agent knows his or her stuff, and is honest and fair. I honestly believe that some of you sellers really don't value these traits! I have lost listings so many times for being honest, but I am always proved right in the end—in fact, I have ended up selling some of those places once the overzealous agent gets canned for, funnily enough, not selling the house.

Most agents would love to be able to offer you their true advice, but are wary of upsetting their clients. So give the agent a chance to voice his or her opinion.

Sold! But which way?

Chapter 11

Deciding on a method of sale

If you're serious about selling your property, you will by now have done ample preparation: you'll have researched your target sales figure; you'll have an idea of which agent you want to sell your place or an alternative method you may want to employ; you'll be serious about selling rather than wasting everybody's time (because you wouldn't do that ... would you?); and you will have prepared your home for sale.

So, it's time to decide how to sell your home: private treaty, auction or tender?

Deciding on a method of sale

I hate to disappoint you, but there is no simple answer to the question of how to sell your home. The method you choose will depend entirely on your circumstances, the market conditions

233

in which you're selling and your personal preference. However, asking yourself a few key questions can help you to decide which option will work best for you.

Is your home in demand?

Whether or not your home is in demand at the time of sale is a key element in any discussion about methods of selling. You will be able to ascertain what level of demand there is for your home by talking to local agents, and by conducting your own market research (see chapter 10 for a detailed discussion of this).

Sometimes you just *know* that when a home hits the market, there will be interested buyers lining up at open inspections. This often happens when the category of home being sold is in low supply but high demand in its market. The high level of demand for a particular property might stem from the fact that the home has features that are rare, in which case availability might be limited. Demand fluctuates constantly, though. The same home at the same price can be in demand one month, and a few months later, it will have greatly reduced demand—so be aware that these things are unpredictable!

Once you have gauged the level of demand, you have options to consider. Agents across Australia all have different opinions on your choices here, but I will give you a good overall guide. Auctions tend to be best for high demand homes, unique or hard-to-value homes and for sales that need to be transparent, so ideal for properties owned by companies or multiple owners. Forced urgent sales also respond well to the focused, time-restrained marketing campaign.

Tender is an alternative to auction and good for many of the reasons an auction is, however it is less popular for no clear reason I can see. It can be less off putting for the more nervous buyers who do not like the public side of an auction.

Private treaty has been and still is the most popular and suitable option for most scenarios; however, very high demand housing and property owned by multiple parties should consider the other two options.

Which sales method has historically been most successful in your area?

The success of each of the three methods—auction, private treaty and tender—will vary substantially from state to state, city to city and even suburb to suburb.

You should generally opt for the method of sale that has been most popular and most successful in your area, while also taking into account your type of housing and what you are comfortable with. If, for example, most homes in your area are sold by private treaty, and only sometimes by auction, I would only suggest going for the auction method if you are very confident that demand for your property is high. As it is an unusual sale method for that area it can run the risk of alienating a proportion of potential buyers who may feel uncomfortable with this process. Likewise, in areas where auctions comprise the majority of home sales with high clearance rates, you should be much more confident in the success of selling at auction. Remember: if you are selling in a good auction environment, even a home that fails to sell at auction has a good chance of selling within the next few weeks, due to the interest generated.

Clearance rates

A clearance rate is the percentage of homes put up for auction that have actually sold under the hammer. It is common for these rates to be calculated over a weekly period for a city or state. Results are published in the local press, and are also available on the major property websites. The figures usually note the sales on the day along with the homes sold after, passed in or not sold. This information is usually free online and also notes the selling agent.

If auction clearance rates are running at less than 50 per cent in your area, you have a 50 per cent chance of failure — not good odds, really! So careful research of the current clearance rates in your area is vital.

To find out how successful a particular method has been in your area, search the 'sold' homes on <www.domain.com.au> and <www.realestate.com.au>. Keep in mind, though, that the price will not always be displayed.

Which sales method do buyers prefer?

In my experience I've found that buyers and sellers are a little like sheep when it comes to their property habits—they don't want to stray off the path of normality!

With this in mind, whatever is considered 'normal' in the local market is often the best path to follow, because buyers will be unlikely to feel intimidated by that method. If you try to sell your house via tender or auction in a market that is dominated by private treaty arrangements, some of the buyers could be scared off.

Similarly, the auction system can scare off buyers who are not used to the format. To undertake an auction in a market that is hostile to auctions, you have to be sure that the demand for your type of home is strong, and that the clearance rates are sturdy enough to counteract the disadvantage at which this method potentially puts you.

How have similar homes been sold?

Let us imagine you are selling a two-bedroom unit. The auction clearance rates in your area are more than 70 per cent, and your agent has suggested an auction. However, having done your own research, you discover that all the homes sold at auction in your suburb have been houses worth two or three times the value of your unit; in fact, no units have been sold by auction successfully for months. In this case, you'd probably be best to ditch the idea of an auction only because the trend in that area currently for selling units is private treaty, so go with what is producing the sales.

Make sure you're comparing apples with apples and take careful note of the published auction results and the home type and number of bedrooms. If there are no two-bedroom units for sale in your area, look at areas nearby. You have to keep abreast of the trends—results any older than a few months are no longer applicable, because the property market moves fast!

Do you have the final say on a sale?

The final decisions about the sale of the home may not be entirely up to one person; often, there are properties where ownership is split between two or more parties. Where multiple ownership is involved, always select auction or tender to avoid hassle. These two methods are the most transparent, because all dealings are out in the open. This reduces the possibility of conflict between parties. Trust me, in all my years of selling houses, the words 'multiple ownership' spell 'guaranteed conflict', unless the sale process is very open. The old marriage break up is often a messy one, and so is the estate of a deceased parent with the feuding offspring. It's generally best to leave the negotiations right out in public.

As a general rule, if a bank or lender has to foreclose and sell a property, they choose to sell the home via auction or tender —regardless of the market preferences. This is because auctions require transparency in the sale negotiations. Public auction is the only clearly visible way to ensure conflicts of interest don't occur. Similarly, tender requires all offers to be considered by all parties involved, reducing the possibility of conflicts of interest or shady dealings. Selling by private treaty can raise the question of 'Could we have not got a higher offer?', as once an offer is accepted, the deal is closed. Whereas selling by auction or tender, buyers are invited to submit their best offer at one time and date.

In addition to answering the questions about your specific scenario, you'll need to get a better understanding about what each different kind of sale involves before making a decision. Each of the three types of sale will be discussed in detail, so read on.

Private treaty

The term 'private treaty' is just the posh phrase for a sale where the terms and dates are completely flexible.

In a private treaty scenario, the real estate agent or seller will advertise the property for sale, usually with a stated price and no set deadlines. The buyer will then submit an offer that outlines their conditions, and the seller will decide to accept, decline or negotiate until the optimum price and conditions are reached for the seller. Generally, a private sale will include the elements discussed in the following pages.

The contract

This sets out the terms and conditions for sale, including deposit requirements and settlement period, title documents, inclusions and exclusions of items within the property and strata and body corporate fees, if appropriate. As a buyer you should seek legal advice before signing any contract to ensure that your interests are being protected. Buying and selling in each state varies, which is a personal gripe of mine! For example, if buying in Queensland, real estate agents can present contracts themselves which can be binding before any lawyer has even had a chance to start his or her hourly rate clicking. My advice is whether buying or selling appoint a legal representative at your earliest opportunity. Sale contracts will have a standardised format in each state and a set procedure, but any contract can have additions or amendments by agreement, so if you have a particular concern you need clarified, just request that concern is addressed. For example, you may insist you sight all paperwork relating to an extension the current owners of the home have undertaken to ensure its compliance with all the local authority requirements.

The cooling off period

This is a specified period of business days after the contracts have been signed, during which the buyer can withdraw their purchase. This is designed to give the buyer time to research their proposed purchase further and obtain building and pest reports—or possibly just time to mull over their choice and change their minds! A warning: a termination penalty can be incurred if as a buyer you withdraw during this period, so read the small print on any disclosures presented to you, or seek legal advice if in doubt. The length of the cooling off period differs from state to state. At the time of publication Western Australia does not offer a cooling off period and other states offer between two and five days. Discuss your rights and obligations under the cooling off period with your lawyer.

For great general information about the legal process for buying and selling, the free information supplied by each state's real estate institute is a great source of independent advice. Visit <www.reiv. com.au> (Victoria); <www.reiwa.com.au> (Western Australia); <www.reinsw.com.au> (New South Wales); <www.reisa.com. au> (South Australia); <www.reiact.com.au> (Australian Capital Territory); <www.reint.com.au> (Northern Territory); <www.reit. com.au> (Tasmania); or <www.reiq.com.au> (Queensland).

Settlement or completion

This is the point at which a buyer becomes the legal owner of the property. The process can be as quick as a week or two, but settlement date is more commonly 30 to 90 days after contracts are initially created and agreed to. On this day, the balance of all monies is paid in exchange for the title to the home. This is a process that takes place between the legal and financial representatives. At this time all outgoings such as rates and services will be adjusted and the lucky new owner will start to owe interest on the new mortgage—hooray!

Is private treaty for me?

There are a number of pros and cons to consider when deciding whether to select the private treaty method. These are described following.

Pros of the private treaty method:

- Private treaty is probably the most common method of sale in Australia, so it feels open to everyone; you alienate none of the buying public. I have yet to meet a buyer who would baulk at a private treaty arrangement.

- You can employ more than one agent at a time when using the private treaty method, if you wish. You may feel comfortable in the knowledge that you have lots of agents who all rush to put the property onto the internet and erect a 'for sale' sign in your beautifully manicured garden. Private treaty is extremely flexible, because it gives you the freedom to chop and change the marketing of your home and to reduce or increase the price; you can even take the property off the market for a few weeks.

- This method gives the seller increased freedom to negotiate with the buyer and agree on whatever terms you require. You could have finally found a buyer but they need to sell another home first so you could allow the transaction to continue subject to the sale of their home if you wanted to.

- This method is suitable for all market conditions.

Cons of the private treaty method:

- As a seller, you may find it frustrating that the buyers will not be held to time restraints. The home is on the market and that is it: no dates are given, so a buyer's urgency is not encouraged.

- Private treaty sellers are less inclined to 'splash the cash', so high-profile marketing campaigns tend not to be used. Also, there is no date restraint with this method so a high-profile campaign may not be viable because your home might be on the market a long period of time.

- The cooling off period could result in you being let down after the deal has been done, making all your hard work seem futile.

🏠 The whole process takes a long time, which is a real downer for some sellers. In private treaties, you have to factor in plenty of time wasting, not to mention extra time for lawyers to fall out with everyone involved, and for one or more of them to spit their proverbial dummy out of the pram!

Private treaty is the most popular of all the methods because it works well for both the buyer and seller in its flexibility. However, the private treaty sale method can end up being long-winded, a bit messy and sometimes darn-right annoying for that very benefit of flexibility!

Auction

An auction is a public sale where buyers bid against each other to buy a property. If the highest bid is acceptable to the seller, a sale is confirmed by the drop of a hammer. The highest bidder signs the contract and pays the deposit at the end of the auction. Exchange of contracts takes place immediately (there is no cooling off period in an auction), and a failure to do so may result in you being pursued by hungry lawyers and hunted down until your assets are all physically removed and your credit cards maxed out. Conditions and procedures for buyers and bidders and the auctioneer vary from state to state.

What's the cost?

There is a common misconception that auctions are prohibitively expensive. This is bizarre, because the only cost involved in choosing an auction over any other method is the cost of hiring the auctioneer (which will usually set you back around $400) — hardly a fortune. The only area with any real potential for cost blowout is the advertising and marketing expenses, as they are generally higher for auctions than all other methods, and are usually paid for by the seller. (See chapter 9 for more on advertising and marketing.)

Is auction for me?

Some of the pros and cons of this selling method are outlined below.

Pros of the auction method:

- A designated date on which the sale must occur means a sense of urgency is encouraged in prospective buyers. This is good for sellers because it encourages buyers to be focused and work to the set date, and the urgency avoids complacency and time for buyers to lose interest.

- If you have hired an agent, there will be an intensive three- or four-week marketing campaign focused on a set date.

- Legal paperwork will be dealt with prior to the auction to avoid delays on the day. The terms and conditions of that contract if the hammer falls are non-negotiable. The advantage is its simplicity. This paperwork is created at the commencement of the proceedings using a combination of seller, agent and lawyer.

- Some buyers love the transparency and ease of the auction method—there's no messing around, and their offers are either accepted or declined on the spot.

- Auctions can foster a sense of competition between buyers, which can encourage them to raise their offers and result in a higher sale price.

Cons of the auction method:

- Agents have a tendency to charge excessively for marketing campaigns when advertising auctions. Also additional auction costs can be incurred such as the auctioneer's fee and possible room hire.

- If the agent has overestimated the level of interest in your house, an auction could be a virtual no-show, or the people that *do* show up might not bid. Any low offers made at auction are recorded, and can be detrimental to future offers. In this case, your home may be blighted in the marketplace.

- The holding of an auction doesn't guarantee that you'll get a sale.

- Buyers may be scared away, perceiving the auction environment as intimidating.

- Sellers have very little flexibility to change their minds if their circumstances change.

- Some buyers expect to get a bargain at an auction, not to pay top dollar. If your house is not in demand, they will act on this expectation by not bidding very high. This could lower the eventual sale price of the home.

To me, deciding on whether to sell at auction is simple: if you are sure that the property is in demand or is something a bit different, you are committed to selling and clearance rates are good, selling by auction is a fantastic option. If you have any doubt about the level of demand for your home, or if you know clearance rates are low, using the auction method may encourage bargain hunters and get you nowhere.

Andrew's hot tip

Try to see the potential auctioneer in action. A dull auctioneer means a dull auction, and it can be vital to get the buyers entertained and wound up to get those offers coming in!

Tender

Tender can take various forms. The basic principle is generally that the seller lists a home and invites offers from prospective buyers, who contact them with proposed terms and conditions by a stated set date. Offers are not legally binding until standard house purchasing contractual conditions have been met. Of course you need to be aware of the protocols in your state but generally you submit your offer and conditions of that offer, and if the seller accepts, off you go. Cooling off is usually involved in these instances as it would be with private treaty and conditions vary state to state.

Is tender for me?

Tender is by far the least popular of the sale methods, but in my humble opinion it is the best, and I would like to see it used a lot more. As buyers like to be comfortable and used to a process popular in their area it might take me a while to convince them. Following are some of the pros and cons of the tender method.

Pros of the tender method:

- Tender doesn't exclude any buyer group, which could increase the number of potential buyers such as people with homes under contract or people wanting long settlements.

- A sense of urgency for buyers to submit an offer by a certain date means a quicker, less hassle-ridden experience for the seller.

- A fixed-term marketing campaign is embarked on, with buyers being told of a set date to submit their offers.

- Sellers are given the flexibility to consider *all* elements of the offers received, not just price, because they have all offers in front of them and it is their decision to make.

- Offers are private, which can benefit the seller because they have time to evaluate all offers, not only the figure, but the terms; for example, a certain settlement date may suit them more than other offers.

- As the closing date is more low key than an auction's date, if the tender process fails to conclude a deal, it is easier to slip back on the market a week or two later, or to negotiate with any interested parties without their full knowledge of previous proceedings.

Cons of the tender method:

- New buyers could be a little scared off by the tender process because they're not familiar with it and may feel that presenting only one 'best' offer could mean they pay too much.

- As with private treaty, the cooling off clause could result in buyers backing out, which can make all the hard work seem futile for sellers.

- Disputes may arise in multi-ownership scenarios, as decisions have to be made jointly by all owners.

- The tender process is not as straightforward as an auction.

In my opinion, tender is the best method because it has the best aspects of all the options: it creates a sense of urgency and competition between buyers like an auction does, but has the flexibility and non-intimidating format of a private sale. Buyers are forced to submit their highest offer straight away, which is great for the seller because it encourages buyers to think high not start low.

Should you provide a price guide?

Buyers generally hate advertisements for homes that do not state a price guide; understandably, they want a clue as to what they're getting in to. I tend to side with the buyers on this one, even if price guides only provide a vague idea about what the home will sell for. Although, I can see the argument for non-pricing too because it means a buyer has to make up their own mind on what it is worth to them. Currently there are no legal obligations to state any kind of figure. Neither should that change if we are to maintain a free market, because all sellers really want the best price.

Let's talk legals

Whether you are selling by auction, tender or private treaty, it is essential that you have a contract prepared by your lawyer before you start marketing your home. Wherever you live, there will be a standardised series of forms. Your lawyer will be able to advise you on how to go about completing these. If you start this as soon as you think about selling, you will avoid annoying delays when you secure a buyer — so get it sorted. Sloppy sellers can end up thousands of dollars in debt, or agreeing to things they don't intend. Ensure the sales contract has the terms you want and is drafted by your lawyer. It will contain elements such as a particular settlement date, the exclusion of pool equipment or your prized lilac hand-woven master bedroom drapes. Some things you as a seller need to clarify for the preparation of the contract are elements that you the current owner will know more about and be able to supply the information to your legal representative. Examples are:

▲ warranties on the building

▲ body corporate/strata fees

▲ permissions for extensions, changes and alterations that you may have made

▲ guarantees on any appliances

▲ inclusions and exclusions offered in the property.

It is so important to get these details right, because if you sign a contract as a buyer or seller, you will be subject to penalties if you fail to comply with the conditions. You cannot foresee the future (can you?) and so you can't predict what kinds of personal or financial problems may arise. You do not want to have to pay another party thousands of dollars if you should default on the contract through no fault of your own, so make sure that the contract protects you as much as possible. Instruct your lawyer to look out for sneaky penalties that a seller or buyer may have included or amended, and which may be completely out of the ordinary. No matter how irrational the penalty may be, if you sign the contract, you will be liable to pay it!

When deciding whether or not to set a price guide, your options are as follows:

- Set an asking price that most people will expect either to pay or to negotiate downwards from. This price attracts buyers; you then hope that if they fall in love with the place, they may start a little lower than the requested figure but work their way up with good old-fashioned negotiating. It really can work. But be warned: stating a price that is too high will be unlikely to attract any inspections whatsoever—trust me: if you price too high, no-one will buy!

- Set a price range (or guide), and expect the final sale amount to fall between those two figures. Price ranges indicate that the seller is flexible, but do not tie the seller to a specific figure. If considerable interest is shown and offers go over, it all feels more acceptable as the price quoted was only a guide.

- Set a minimum price. If you are in a forced sale scenario, stating a competitive price will attract deal seekers because they know you are serious about selling. Sometime this low figure attracts so much interest buyers can start to compete and a good selling price is actually achieved. Everyone starts low but has to go up!

- Don't disclose a price at all. I personally do not like the no-pricing option, however it is quite common and understandable in auction sales—even though it makes me uncomfortable. It does have some merits. Agents tell me the 'no price disclosed' policy works well for many, but buyers tell me they hate unpriced homes. No pricing allows freedom for the seller to seek an offer without constraints of stating a figure, but some buyers do not want to play the game. This does not necessarily encourage higher figures, and can frustrate all parties, as no-one knows what anyone wants. Non-pricing seems to be much more common in cases where a property is unique and there are no sales to judge the price against.

Remember that all options are reasonably successful in different circumstances.

. . . .

What's the agent thinking?

Agents love auctions, as they generate so much advertising and enquiries—all of it around their brand (and likely paid for by the seller). So keep this in mind when you're deciding what selling method to go for. Just because the agent is heartily encouraging you to go to auction doesn't mean it's the best way to go!

The dream home

Chapter 12

*What's the agent
looking for?*

As an agent, you learn pretty quickly that some houses are much easier to sell than others are. Although there are factors—such as market conditions—that can affect the likelihood of selling, the single biggest factor in a home's saleability is the willingness of the seller to adhere to a few basic guidelines.

Yes, I know—you're already thinking that you don't need to worry about this stuff, because your home will be a dream to sell! After all, it is gorgeous, and you have such impeccable taste! Moreover, you have converted your formal lounge room into a media room; your kitchen refit cost a *fortune* in 1993; and you have had your windows heavily tinted. The home is *perfect* for all those buyers out there who need a sewing room and a formal dining room for their dogs. You are sure that your place truly is going to be an easy sell, so you don't bother doing any research on who your market is, and you don't contemplate making any adjustments to your home.

Let me enlighten you. If you could flash forward six months, this is what you'd see: one failed auction, three big price reductions, and so many agents involved in the selling process that you no longer need to hand out a key—you just leave all the doors unlocked day and night! The weekly updates from agents have stopped due to lack of interest, and the house is buried at the bottom of the property websites, as new properties get entered onto the website leaving yours to languish at the end of the listings, only to be discovered by mistake. The open inspections have ceased, and the few inspections you *do* get are an obvious attempt by agents to get the buyers to purchase something else! (Yes, you may be disheartened to hear this will happen, but if your property has not sold and a similar property comes onto the market, your agent may well use your property to make the other one look good.)

So how can you avoid getting into this predicament? And, more importantly, how can you make *your* house the dream home every agent wants to sell?

What defines a really saleable home?

In order to ensure your home is as saleable as possible, you need to combine a number of elements. The most important of these are:

- the right product
- the right price
- the right market conditions
- the right strategy for promoting your property.

Having all four of these elements working for you is a winning combination.

Why property developers get the winning combo

Large, high-profile property developers often succeed in selling properties having achieved only three of the four elements listed. There are several reasons for this.

Developers can employ high-profile marketing agencies. These marketers research what buyers actually want, and adapt the product accordingly.

While it is almost impossible to *create* the desired market for your property, sometimes developers release stock at the best possible time in the market's cycle.

Developers can afford to spend huge amounts of money on advertising. Think about how much you could personally spend on advertising your home, and then imagine how much you could spend if you got together with your neighbours and split a new budget between 40 or 50 of you. That is all developers do — they have 25, 50, maybe 100 homes, blocks or units to promote, so the cost per home is minimal but the impact is amazing!

Developers can often fail to offer a product at the right price. This is because they have studied and invested in ensuring all the other factors are adhered to — they can push those prices up as high as they like if it is the only element being ignored — the buyers will bite!

Making sure you have the right product

It can be hard to ascertain whether or not you have the right product (or the right home, as the case may be). Often, the 'right' product will depend on what consumers want at a particular time. To make things even harder, the nature of the product (housing) does not lend itself to changing to match market conditions. For example, if you're selling a block of land that you can't afford to build on, there's nothing you can do to tailor your product to the market. Likewise, if you are selling a big family home in an area where everyone wants small townhouses, you are not in a position to change the product. You do, however, have *some* power to 'give the buyer what they want'—but only within the parameters of your existing dwelling.

So, what can you do? To put it simply, you can try and work out who your buyers are—that is, their possible age group, numbers in the household, and so on—and then you present your home in such a way as to appeal to that market. I've given two examples of how this can work following.

The DINK couple

You and your partner have a large three-bedroom home located in a suburb in which many young families are buying housing. However, you are a young and trendy couple who couldn't think of anything worse than a few ankle biters encroaching on your socialising, footy and surfing time. Your home, in this scenario, has not been used as a three-bedroom family home, but rather a one-bedroom, one-gym, one-high-tech-study-with-(tasteful)-nude-photos-liberally-adorning-the-walls home. The issue here is that your target buyers are most probably young families, not other DINK (dual-income-no-kids) couples. If you are aware of this, it's within your power to make your house into a three-bedroom family style home. You just need to ensure that each room can be easily converted to its 'family style' purpose—you can even go so far as to borrow furniture and other 'props' from your friends and relatives to make the study into a nursery. If you give buyers what they want, they will buy. And they will be more generous with their dollars than you think!

'Dude, your house is, like, sooooooo mid '90s'

You have owned your home for 15 years, and you modernised it back when you first purchased. On talking to selected real estate agents you discover that the target market for your house are younger buyers who will think your home is, like, *soooo* mid '90s! In this case, it's time to paint the lime-green-and-purple kitchen cupboards white, and 'get with the noughties' for the best selling price. Adapt your product a little.

Of course, if you're really not interested in doing some work on your product to make it just right for the buyers, you just have to be sure that the other three elements are spot-on … and that definitely means that the price has to come down.

Making sure you pick the right price

As we discovered in the previous chapter, setting the price for your property is entirely in your control. However, setting the price is a tricky issue, and getting the price right could take a few attempts (especially if you're disclosing a figure when you advertise). With the correct market research, you have the power to get it right. If you are not disclosing an asking price when you advertise and you are receiving offers, you need to listen to those figures and see if they tie-in with your research, so if they get close whip that contract out! Pricing is an element that can have a huge negative or positive impact on your ability to sell your home. However, you can deal with it whenever you decide you are ready to. I know for many people that takes quite a while! Strategies vary not disclosing a figure and it's a risky approach, but it will let buyers express their feelings towards the property good or bad — remember they will always start low. If it fails and no offers come in, it is time to state a price. You can state a price in various forms as explained in previous chapters, but the trick is not to start too high — this will scare buyers away.

Making sure you are in the right market

The property market is a complicated and fragile thing, and it can change within the blink of an eye. Unfortunately, the market's condition at the specific time that you want (or need) to sell is something that you have no control over. When selling in a good market (when there is a high demand for a product like yours, but a limited supply), a sale will be easy, and you'll be likely to get a good price for your home. If the property market is bad (low demand and high supply of properties like the one you're selling), you either need to get all elements other than price so spot on that market conditions cease to be an issue, or play the waiting game and hit the market when you think the time is right.

The media (bless 'em) often comments on the property market, and when is a good time to buy or sell. Unfortunately, they are often wrong.

Ignoring the media and hype, here are a few ways to find out whether the market is right:

- local agents will be begging for listings—with promises of many cashed-up buyers

- there will be a reduced number of 'for sale' boards around, and a high number of 'sold' signs

- there will be low levels of stock for sale, and sales happening quickly all around you

- real estate magazines and real estate sections of the press will carry less pages of property advertising

- direct mail will increase with agents' new listings and invites to view new properties on the market

- large franchise groups of real estate agents will hit the TV and radio networks selling the benefits of their brand.

Similarly, you can spot the signs of a bad market if you watch carefully. Some of these signs include:

- agents will appear cautious in valuations and expectations and not chase listings where the seller's motivation is 'to test the water'

- the neighbourhood will be littered with numerous sale boards that are starting to show signs of weathering

- half your suburb is for sale and the sales you hear about ended with the seller 'giving it away'

- catchy headings such as 'Liquidation sale', 'Desperate owner needs to sell' and 'Owner has moved interstate' show a sign of desperation, as does the heading 'Make an offer'.

So getting this element right is all about your ability to *read* the market; you have no control on this one!

Making sure you have the right promotion

Ensuring that you have the right strategy for marketing your home can actually have a major impact on your ability to sell for a price you're happy with—even if your budget is tight.

Following are some tips that will help you to promote your property effectively.

Find out what your market wants

Finding out what your market wants is all about knowing what buyers are likely to get excited about. You can research this by talking to local agents who have been active in your area, reading the property editorial of your local press and looking through glossy magazines to show interior and exterior design trends. Having done some research, you should ask yourself these questions about the prospective buyers who comprise your target market:

- What features will they want?
- What house type do they prefer?
- What are they looking for in terms of location?
- What lifestyle options are they interested in?

If you can answer them effectively, you will be much closer to understanding who your target market is, and therefore be able to tailor your product to their needs.

Selectively promote aspects of your home that will appeal to your market

Target the right buyers by promoting the aspects of your home that they want to see. To do this, you have to play on your property's strengths. Selectively promote the features that will excite buyers, or play up the features of your home that will give it an edge over the competition.

But be careful! Legally, you really cannot lie about any fundamental feature of your home, and if you exaggerate or make massive false statements in your advertising, you are shooting yourself in the 'for sale' board. Even if you do try to lie about your home's features, you will soon be found out: hidden structural problems will be discovered when the buyer has the building inspection done; and a property's location cannot be faked. In fact, courtesy of Google Earth you can even see if the home you're planning to inspect is situated next to a service station or chemical waste processing plant before you even leave your desk.

I still see agents and private sellers alike making ridiculous claims about a property, and it really does not help in the sales process — it gives the agent a bad name, too! Instead of lying, try using humour and honesty to entice buyers — it generally works really well.

Know how to reach the right buyers

When choosing advertising formats or deciding where to advertise, always keep the possible target market in mind. The average Aussie property only needs to be promoted locally via an agent's database, ads in the local property supplements and websites. Other options available are glossy lifestyle coffee table magazines or direct marketing. Some of the large franchise offices produce their own magazines that are sent to local hotels and a select group of clients. Do not forget that if the agent is highly proactive in the immediate area, he or she will be known and trusted for his or her judgement.

Although sellers only really need to promote locally, they can now reach potential buyers all over the world via the internet (as long as buyers are searching for their particular suburb or surrounds, of course).

Do not waste money on advertisements in print media unless it is used by local buyers. Advertisements on random websites or in the *Australian Butchers Monthly* are not likely to hit the right target! Most people interested in buying will look at advertisements in the local property publications, because buyers don't want to decide, or commit, until they have seen what else is on offer.

Always speak the truth

Recently, a home near mine was advertised as being '15 minutes from the CBD'. In reality, it is about 35 kilometres from the CBD. That means you would have to travel at a constant speed of about 130 kilometres per hour the whole way, not stopping for junctions or lights, and *certainly* not slowing down for corners, oncoming traffic or speed signs. Any police vehicles would just have to be passed by with a polite wave. A 15-minute trip to the CBD would be added to by detention in a police cell, providing you had actually made it without crashing the car. Imagine that a serious buyer takes the advertisement literally! They could have liked the home, but this big lie could actually just annoy them. Not conducive to doing a deal, is it?

So play to your property's *genuine* strengths; there will surely be plenty. If the home needs work, be honest about it in the advertisements.

Generally, the dream home to sell is the one where the price is right. Often these will be homes requiring renovation, because they are cheaper than most of the other homes in that area. Alternatively, the best homes to sell are the ones that are extremely well presented. In these cases, the homes will be a little above average on price, but they are worth it because of the style and features they offer. The rest of the housing stock needs to adhere to our four rules: right product; right price; right market conditions; and right promotion—or at least three of them! If you don't adhere to these rules, expect to be on the market a long time!

. . . .

What's the agent thinking?

If you want get an agent excited, give him or her a listing in the 'best house to sell' category. All agents love that—and why wouldn't they? The product is ready for the market, and the only challenge will be negotiating a good price and sorting serious buyers from the tyre kickers!

I recall the first dream home I ever sold—the experience is one that has shaped my property career ever since. It was 1984; I was a young trainee real estate agent, and had been left to act as agent for a real estate office during the manager's annual summer holidays (after just six months in the profession, mind you!).

I was lucky enough to have the help of the receptionist, Jane—a lovely woman of around pension age, I thought at the time (that is, she was in her mid 20s), who smoked the whole way through every conversation we had. Her local knowledge was essential, as I had only been to the suburb in which the office was located a few times in my life. I was 17, had no knowledge of recent sales in the area, no understanding of what local buyers would be looking for, and could barely even locate the office on the first day. It was a recipe for disaster.

A few days into my time there, I took a phone call from someone wanting to sell their home. They had other agents biting at their ankles, but wanted us to pitch for their business. I was very excited, but played hard to get and said I would not be able to inspect their home for at least 10 to 15 minutes, as I was busy emptying my colleague's ashtray.

The first thing Jane asked me when I got off the phone was, 'Did you get any info on the house?'

'Yes,' I replied, 'they said it was all done up.' To that, Jane warned me that just because a seller says their house is 'all done up', doesn't mean it is even sellable. She told me to try not to talk exact values with the sellers on the spot, and said we could have a discussion about the potential sale price on my return.

So I got into my shiny company car, drove the 0.75 km to the house, pulled up outside, and decided it looked like all the others in the street.

But inside, it was a different story. After the shaking of the hands with the owners (all the while noticing they were staring at me, probably wondering whether school had got out early that day), they gave me a guided tour of their classic turn-of-the-century two-storey English terrace. As I walked from room to room, my jaw got closer to the ground; the hairs on the back of my neck, had I had any at that stage of my life, would have been standing up.

After the tour, the owners enquired as to my opinion of their home. Of course, in my naivety I forgot everything I had discussed with Jane, and squealed out something to the effect of, 'Your house is fantastic, it is sooo cool, wow, I love it!'

Their next question, of course, was 'What do you think we can get?' I just blurted out a figure—$80 000, if I recall. The owners looked at each other, looked at me and immediately replied, 'If you think we can get that figure, you can have the exclusive listing, young man!'

I strutted back into the office, and Jane looked up. 'Well?' she enquired.

I told Jane the full story, and she was very impressed. 'But how did you manage to avoid talking prices? Shall we work out a figure now?'

'Umm … well … I kind of forgot that we were going to discuss it later, and told them I thought we could get $80 000.'

'What?! Are you mad?' she exploded.

'What's wrong? Is that a little toppy, then?'

'Nothing ever sells in that street for more than $70 000 — usually $60 000 to $68 000 is the normal range. What are we going to do?'

Not fazed by this, I decided there was only one option: get on the phone and call all buyers looking in the area (despite none of those listed having budgets of more than $70 000). Amazingly, within the first few days I met a buyer at the property, and …

… they purchased the house at the full asking price. (How could they not, with a squeaky, skinny 17-year-old telling them it was the best house they would ever see?)

The point of the story is that a house that is easy to sell really is worth its weight in gold. And if you have one of these top-of-the-range houses, expect the agents to fight over your listing. Play hard to get! The agents might be willing to negotiate a better deal for you just to secure the listing.

Final thoughts

The great Aussie dream

If you have managed to get to the end of the book and are now reading the conclusion, it is pretty safe to say that you love houses as much as I do! I have to confess that one of the main reasons that I came to Australia is because of a dream — my dream, it turns out, is also the great Australian dream: to own my own little piece of Australia.

The great Aussie dream has always centred on our desire to own our own home. In the last 50 years or so, this dream has been within reach of more Australians than ever before because of the unprecedented availability of finance. This has fuelled an even greater demand for housing, and the market has continued to grow steadily. As a result, properties have continued to appreciate in value, and many people have made a lot of money from owning property. Our property market has a history of long-term growth, and buying and selling property has become an integral part of the modern Australian lifestyle.

The foundation of the Australian housing market is its strength and stability. Australian and overseas investors consider it is a safe place to invest—not bad for a country with a relatively young property market and a population that's tiny by global standards!

Aussie housing stock

The Australian property market is full of diversity and opportunity. In exchange for some of your hard-earned cash, you can purchase a tiny urban apartment surrounded by chic coffee shops and boutiques in the midst of the hustle and bustle of city life. Or, for the same amount of money, you can get a country cottage surrounded by 10 acres of your own land that's full of peace, tranquillity and natural beauty. Alternatively, there's a huge demand for the all-Aussie beach lifestyle, where you can buy a house only a few hundred metres from the ocean. If you just want to live in a suburban street with a nice backyard, or a townhouse where you and your neighbours meet around a great community pool, you can have that, too. These are real choices—not just for the rich, but also for the average Aussie. It is all out there!

Australian housing stock is as diverse architecturally as it is in terms of location. Housing stock that was built prior to the '50s is rare, and, as such, is often preserved for its heritage value. The '50s heralded a new era for housing design and, along with many other countries in the world, Aussies really did all lose the architectural plot in this period! We didn't come to our senses again until the late '80s, and during this time we saw the construction of some absolute architectural shockers, sporting features such as yellow-tinted glass, super-low ceilings, flat roofs and disappearing verandas. Unfortunately, that era was a time of huge construction for Australia, so there are still some of these monstrosities on the market today. On the positive side, many of these homes (well, those not constructed using asbestos, of course) were very solidly built. Many of them occupy prime blocks in prime urban locations where land is at a premium. Do not be put off by these architectural curiosities—they can be regenerated into attractive, modern and liveable homes; you just have to be creative. A modernised, remodelled home from this era can be a great home for the noughties.

Housing stock has changed dramatically in recent decades and hopefully will continue to evolve in the right direction. Between the mid '90s and the mid noughties an unprecedented number of new homes were created. According to the Australian Bureau of Statistics, a total of 1 218 458 new homes were created between 1996 and 2006, with units being the biggest housing type to increase.

The size of our average Aussie home has also been getting bigger, while block size has decreased in urban areas and suburbs in which low-cost housing is being developed.

The future of the housing market

The Australian housing market is built on strong foundations: a strong banking system with four of the major Australian banks now constituting four of only 11 among the world's largest 100 banks to be rated AA or above. Also we have a population with a desire to own property. Based on the history of the housing market, it can be inferred that owning residential property offers an almost cast-iron guarantee of long-term profit. (Although, as we all know, that profit can vary from 'Why did I bother' to 'Oh my God, I am off to order a yacht!') Australians believe that owning property will allow them to create wealth for the future, so the housing market always fights its way back from its lowest points.

For those faced with the possibility of selling at a loss, make sure that you assess all your possible options as history dictates that time is on your side: as long as you can afford to retain the dwelling, the market will eventually readjust itself in your favour, so just hang in there if you can.

Investing in property should be a simple process, and you should be able to retain full control. The principle here is to use your common sense and conduct careful research. Wait until market conditions are favourable to buyers, then look to purchase a property in a location that shows promising potential for growth. When it comes time to sell, hopefully demand for your property will be up, and supply down—so you can sell for a profit.

Future growth areas are hard to predict, and you should be wary of experts claiming to be able to predict the next 'hot spot'. Genuine growth areas are governed by employment opportunities, business opportunities, business projects and access to amenities, or alternatively by the expansion of a neighbouring suburb—a chain reaction starts, and population growth and property values rise. When trying to predict these future growth areas for the purpose of investing, it's important to be aware that finding a few nuggets of gold in a creek and chucking up a few tents doesn't constitute the next Pleasantville. When you hear developers screaming that a certain place is *the next big thing,* check that this is really a tangible scenario. When buying housing in future growth areas, remember that it has to be *cheaper* than established safer areas, or you may as well just buy in an established suburb and avoid any risk!

So it's fair to say that I have great faith in the future of the Australian housing market. However, there are a few things that I would love to see improve.

I would love to see the government wake up, see sense and nationalise the house-buying legal process with one set of rules for all states. It would be great for the public, as well as for the whole industry, as there are so many anomalies between the states regarding contract procedures, the rules around cooling off periods and other issues.

I have watched quite a few buying eras come and go and I want first homebuyers to understand that to get the Aussie dream you may have to compromise on a few things at first, just to get a foot in the door. Most people can afford a mortgage but cannot afford the four fully maxed credit cards, the car loan, a season ticket for the footy and the vast amount of high-tech gadgetry that is so 'essential'. Compromise and buy a first home that you can reasonably afford, then after many years of ownership sell it with a bit of profit allowing you to buy the next home with less compromise. I would love homebuyers to stop being obsessed with getting a great deal or caring about what other people think and remember that they are supposed to be buying a house that they will love and want to call their home.

I would also like to see the end of dodgy third-party marketeers selling so called 'deals' to investors that are not deals at all. Likewise, I would like to see those investors who get sucked in by dodgy marketeers stop being lazy, use their brains and do a bit more research — then the marketeers would simply be out of business.

The final item on my wishlist is for agents to be given a bit of a break. There really are so many good ones out there. Similar to any service industry, instead of complaining about the whole profession just ditch the bad agents and hire the good ones. A good agent should work with you, know your likes and dislikes and save you time and money by finding you that dream home.

The future of Australian real estate is strong. I have really only scratched the surface of this vast and fascinating subject in this book, but I hope you have now realised that real estate and property investment are not a mystery, and to be successful in this market you just need to do your research and use your common sense. And remember: time will heal most property mistakes, so continue to buy and sell and live in our Aussie homes … just please don't park on your front lawn!

Happy buying and selling!

Index